BACKSTAGE AT SATURDAY NIGHT LIVE!

An Unauthorized Portrait

MICHAEL McKENZIE

with photos by Edie Baskin

SCHOLASTIC BOOK SERVICES
New York Toronto London Auckland Sydney Tokyo

Ken Regan/Camera 5 — back cover photos and front cover photos of Bill Murray, John Belushi, and Dan Aykroyd.
Globe Photos — Gilda Radner (front cover).

ISBN 0-590-30919-6

 Published by Scholastic Book Services, a division of Scholastic Magazines, Inc.

12 11 10 9 8 7 6 5 4 3 2 1 2 0 1 2 3 4 5/8
Printed in the U.S.A. 06

ACKNOWLEDGMENTS

Special Thanks to Dr. Steve Ryan for technical assistance.

Dedicated to the here and now, especially to Robert Creeley who said, "Here is where there is." This, after all, is the geometry of need, an illumination, funny.

To Chevy, John & Dan who moved to keep things whole.
To Gilda who is Peter Pan.
To Bill who never stops.
To Laraine who makes corduroys look good.
To Jane, completely abstract.
And for Garrett, a wise guy.

CONTENTS

★ ★ ★ ★ ★ ★ ★ ★ ★ ★ ★ ★ ★ ★ ★ ★ ★ ★

Backstage at Saturday Night Live!

In early 1975, Lorne Michaels, a 29-year-old Canadian writer and television producer, presented an idea for a new television show to the people in charge of programming at NBC. Michaels had strong feelings about television and wanted to produce a show that was fresh and young, one created by and aimed at the people in this country who had grown up with television. Michaels felt that both the proposed creators and the intended audience wanted something different on TV, something a little more contemporary, more humorous, and perhaps a bit irreverent. Michaels wasn't particularly interested in controversial political issues — that was too heavy. It wasn't even sex, although a show that reflected the youth of the country might be a little more daring than Lawrence Welk. But he knew that networks were large corporations, with a sharp eye on profits and great fears about the possibility of offending anyone in their vast audience. What Michaels wanted was humor: fast, hip, topical, and silly. If rock music came of age in the Sixties, then the Seventies would be the age of the big laugh. The young, hip, *television* comic.

Michaels had thought about this show for a long time. But it took him a while to convince the network to back him up. "I had studied and sat in on the *Monty Python* series," recalls Michaels, "and I had a sense of the kind of television I wanted to do. Every time I attempted to do it in Los Angeles during prime time [the hours between 8 and 11 P.M., the most important, expensive, and heavily viewed hours], I was told that no one would understand what I was doing. They said I was 'too inside' and even if a small minority could understand the 'in' jokes, a majority wouldn't. About the same time, I produced the *Lily Tomlin Special*. The

Michael O'Donoghue clowns with Lorne Michaels. Their definition of "experimental TV" and the network's were two different things. (Edie Baskin/NBC)

network tested this show before it was broadcast and they didn't like the results. Later, much later, I got an Emmy for it. Actually, however, what is proved to me was that I couldn't work in prime-time television."

But Michaels persisted with his idea for a new show anyway. He eventually found a receptive ear in NBC's new head of late-night programming. He was ready to experiment. Michaels was asked to produce 40 shows and a pilot program. (A pilot is a show produced to introduce a new series. It is used to test viewer reaction and create anticipation for the new show.) But Michaels refused! He wouldn't do a pilot because he felt he needed time to work out his ideas and a pilot wouldn't be a very good example of what the show would be like.

Michaels and NBC argued back and forth about the "Show Without a Pilot." NBC needed a really good reason for going ahead and Michaels, in a moment of true genius, gave them one they couldn't refuse: he would broadcast the show *live*, from New York! It was perfect for Michaels *and* NBC. But better for Michaels:

"Listen, if this show had been seen before," recalls Michaels, "it would never have gone on the air. Not that we were doing anything illicit, really. Just that my definition of 'experimental television' and the network's were two different things."

When Michaels finally won his point—skipping the pilot—the Great Saturday Night Search was on. He had six months to put a show together and a world to cover to do it. But he knew where to start. He had previously worked in Toronto with Gilda Radner and Danny Aykroyd, who performed with a comedy troupe known as Second City. He held mass auditions to fill out the rest of the cast. Of the seven original cast members (Aykroyd, Belushi, Chase, Curtin, Morris, Newman, and Radner), only Jane Curtin was chosen on the basis of her audition. Chevy Chase, appropriately, had the strangest entrance to Michaels' tribe: they met on line at a Monty Python movie.

Fall guy Chevy Chase (right) had the strangest entrance into Michaels' tribe. (Rain Worthington)

There are few popular myths about the show. First, contrary to what most people think, it was never a "low budget" show. Lorne Michaels had enough experience in TV to understand how important an adequate budget is to a show's success. He demanded and received $150,000 per show, a very good amount.

Another popular rumor is that all the performers and writers were originally connected to the National Lampoon, a bunch of "crazy kids." Not true. With the exception of Belushi, Michael O'Donoghue, and a couple of writers, the team was mostly television or theater professionals with some of whom Michaels had worked before. Again, Michaels insisted on top professionals, all around. Even his technical crew—the cameramen, soundmen, and others—were handpicked for their experience and excellence. After all, doing a live, 90-minute show every week is hardly a cinch for pros, let alone amateurs.

At long last, *SNL* had an entire army, led by The Not Ready for Prime Time Players. On October 11, 1975, with George Carlin as the first guest host (another innovation that guaranteed variety), *Saturday Night* was broadcast for the first time. It was an instant success, winning the ratings game with an audience of five million viewers.

Despite criticism from corners that found the show too offensive, watching *SNL* gradually became the "in" thing to do on Saturday night. People all over the country were coming home early, or staying up late to watch the Not Ready For Prime Time Players perform their craziness.

It didn't take long for *SNL* to become a certified hit. By the middle of the first season, it was the biggest draw on late-night television. Part of the show's success was and is due to discovering new comics, actors, and rock stars, and putting them before a national audience. The dean of late night TV, Johnny Carson, was the master of 'showcasing' new talent, an idea that worked equally well for *SNL*. *SNL* became *the* place to see the new stars, first. And young America tuned in.

At the end of the first season, the cast was asked to make a personal appearance in Houston, Texas, in June, 1976, and it would be the first time they had

George Carlin guest-hosted the first *SNL* show to over 5,000,000 viewers. (Edie Baskin/NBC)

played before a large, live audience (The studio audience numbers only 300 persons). Larry Gray, then *SNL* publicity director, remembers, "We expected a big turn-out, three or four thousand. It was to kick off the fall fashion line of a huge department store down there. We got involved with them and the entire cast, minus Chevy, went down. We originally figured that we'd do a sort of question and answer session with the people, since everyone in the cast was into improvisation anyway. We ended up doing an actual performance, after a short rehearsal; there were over 20,000 people in the audience. It was the first time the cast had any direct knowledge of their huge appeal. Now they were out in the street, with a large crowd cheering, "LARAINE!" "GILDA!" "JOHN BEL-USH-I." I mean, you couldn't believe it! The crowd was cheering like mad, screaming and howling. It was great.

"I remember we were all packed into one limousine after the show. Wall to wall people the entire way to the airport. Everyone was stunned, really. Sure, the

Jane gives Gilda a dubious look on "Weekend Update." (Edie Baskin)

cast had all played in theaters before but nothing like this. We all realized the full power of television, to reach people, 28,000 people, in a place you had never even been! Suddenly, Gilda made the comment, "Boy, I think we're the Beatles of comedy!" and indeed that was the feeling that everyone now *had* to be aware of. It was an interesting moment to be with these people, when they fully realized the actual power of what they were doing."

But the popularity of the show has created some problems few had foreseen. Individuals, like Chevy

As was the case with Chevy, the incredible popularity of The Blues Brothers literally forced them off the show. (Atlantic Records)

Chase, who became instant celebrities, were forced by public demand to seek wider audiences for their talents. Chase was given a contract to create television specials and has appeared in movies. He starred in *Foul Play* with Goldie Hawn, and will star in the new Benji movie called *Oh, Heavenly Dog!*

"I'm Chevy Chase...and you're not." (Edie Baskin/NBC)

Gilda Radner says, "When Chevy first started to get famous, my mother used to ask what he was like. Then, when he got real famous, she started asking me what he had for lunch, like instead of what *I* had for lunch. Then, when he got really, *really* famous, she began to doubt that I even knew him at all."

Lorne Michaels has a different point of view: "It's a grueling job. There's no time for a private life. That's why Chevy left." Chase, himself, offers a third version: "Doing *SNL* is like picking fruit or doing some other kind of manual labor that exhausts you. It's a high-tension existence that works against the need for relaxation and looseness." About being considered by many a "star" of the show, Chevy observes, "It felt funny being the one that was singled out for all the praise knowing that everyone was breaking their backs, just as I was."

Despite Chase's exit, the show continued to become more and more popular. Aykroyd and Belushi, and Bill Murray, who became a permanent member of the cast in 1977, Gilda Radner, and the others stepped into the vacuum left by Chevy and more than filled it. Unfortunately, unparalleled success may be the show's downfall.

Danny Aykroyd and John Belushi quit the show in the fall of 1979. Their popularity propelled them into the more inviting and glamorous world of movies. With the huge success they won for their Blues Brothers act, a motion picture was inevitable, and hence a loss to the show.

Gilda Radner has performed a successful one-woman Broadway show. Will she stay and work like a demon on *SNL* if greener pastures beckon?

Lorne Michaels has had luck and foresight in choosing guest hosts and musical acts.

On October 23, 1976, *Saturday Night Live!* unleashed on the world that wiiiillld & crr-aaazzy guy,

On October 23, 1976, *SNL* unleashed that wiiiillld & crazy guy, Steve Martin, on all our funnybones. (Rain Worthington)

Steve Martin. Like Lorne Michaels, Martin had won an Emmy as a writer for the Smothers Brothers. But no one could have imagined how well Martin worked with all the *SNL* players. And, for that matter, how well Martin would go over with fans of all ages. "I had no idea the 'Czech Brothers' would be as popular as they are," shrugs Dan Aykroyd. "Steve had a character called 'Continental Suave Guy.' I saw him do it in his act one night and I really enjoyed it. I went backstage afterward and I said, 'Listen, Steve, I "do" this Czech architect . . .' I'd noticed a tremendous similarity in the rhythms of Steve's character and I said, 'Let's put them both together as Czechs who wear polyester shirts and everything!' It didn't work that well with the studio audience the first time we did it on the show. But we got so much feedback from people who watched it on TV, phew!!!, it really blew me away."

Nearly every major band from the current crop of New Wave rockers has appeared on *SNL*. Not surprisingly, their stars rose noticeably after their appearance. Patti Smith, for example, appeared on the show when she was still relatively unknown. Barely 18 months later, her album *Easter* soared up the charts and she was featured on the cover of *Rolling Stone* magazine. *SNL* clearly exerts a strong influence on the tastes of younger people.

But with continued defections from the cast, and a limited number of new musicians worthy of the attention, how long can *SNL*'s popularity last? Can Michaels continue to find new stars every few months? The show is ground-breaking for television. It will be imitated, modified, idolized, patronized, and put down. It will be cited by both critics and advocates of a looser style of television. But mainly, in true television form, it will be imitated. Probably the other networks have scripts, casts, and pilots being prepared at the present moment.

But one thing that can never be easily duplicated is the human element that is so crucial to *SNL*'s success:

the people who write, act, and produce this crazy quilt of a show. There is only one Not Ready for Prime Time Players, for better or worse.

***SNL* has become *the* place for new talent in both comedy and music to reach millions. Patti Smith was the first New Wave act featured on the show. (Michael McKenzie)**

★ ★ ★ ★ ★ ★ ★ ★ ★ ★ ★ ★ ★ ★ ★ ★ ★ ★

Live From New York!

Studio 8H at 30 Rockefeller Center has a long history of contributing to television history. It was the home of the legendary conductor, Toscanini, the original home of *The Tonight Show,* and many others. Because of its history, and the fact that it is NBC's largest television studio area, Michaels wheeled and dealed to secure it as the home of *Saturday Night Live.* And although *SNL* may never produce anything more "important" than parodies of various presidents nor anyone closer to a virtuoso than the Blues Brothers, you can bet two tickets to a dress rehearsal that old Studio 8H never had so many jokes cracked inside its walls in its whole life.

My first tour of 8H was on the first day of rehearsal for show #73, to be aired on December 2, 1978. It was a Wednesday, the first day the cast meets with writers and technicians for "read-throughs" of the skits. I arrived before most of the crew. Studio 8H looks like a huge high-school auditorium twisted around so that the stage becomes the long side, rather than the short. The atmosphere is calm, almost serious. A few people are walking around or sitting and reading their skits. I

Studio 8H: NBC's largest television studio and home of *SNL*. (Dr. Steve Ryan)

could never have anticipated the high-speed madness that would soon follow.

By about one o'clock in the afternoon, everyone is on the set, and you have to watch what you're doing or you'll walk into any one of a thousand wrong places. There are now about 60 people in the studio: cameramen, stars, lighting crews, stage hands, costume people, technical crews—all crucial to the making of the show, all responsible in one way or another for the success, or failure, of the now $250,000-a-week production.

The look of the show on Wednesday is very loose, something like a group of kids at a picnic. The guys wear dungarees and either tee shirts or collared button-downs, while the women are dressed colorfully, chewing gum and giggling. On the surface, it doesn't look much different than a dozen things anyone has done, and it looks as if the cast and crew are not even aware of the fact that in three days all of this is going to be seen by about 40 million people. But by the time Saturday rolls around you realize that producing one show of *Saturday Night Live!* is like taking all your final exams and the college boards in 90 hair-raising minutes!

Bill Murray, *SNL*'s resident nerd, must have been born in sneakers and a sweatshirt. You watch him bop around the set with "joker" written all over his face. He wouldn't give noogies to the cameraman, would he? *Absolutely!* He pixies right over to the wary cameraman, who immediately shields his noggin with his hands. Bill throws him a little wink. "Oh, you're wise to me, huh? Not bad. You're a slob. I mean, all this mustard all over your tie. Really...." The cameraman immediately steps back, jerks his head, and covers his nose. Murray gives him a wide-eyed look of surprise. "Oh, you're wise to that one too." Then Bill takes a half step away, as if he's going to leave. Immediately pivoting back, Murray grabs at the cameraman's top pocket. "Hey, I didn't know you smoked cigars...." The cameraman goes to slap at Murray's hand but before he can say, "C'mon Bill, leave my cig..." Murray strikes! He flips a finger right up to the guy's beak and dances away laughing.

Bill Murray is the Resident Nerd, Noogie Master, and Goofball Extraordinaire both on and off camera. Here Gilda gets her daily dose. (Edie Baskin)

As the day goes on, the pace picks up and the script is getting worked over, tested, rewritten, and learned. It becomes increasingly evident that the show is a collaborative effort in a real sense with the writers, stars, designers, and technical people continually bouncing ideas off each other and acting as each other's audience. It is not unusual for a cameraman or a set designer to make a suggestion, have it welcomed by the writer of the skit, and used on the show. The writers talk in a non-stop, machinegun-like manner, which can really wear you thin after a while. Within a few hours you get the picture: if you're going to hang around the studio, you're going to be put to use as a trial audience for the tons of jokes piling up in everyone's head.

On each day of production, a schedule is given to everyone concerned with the show. It includes a breakdown of which skits will be rehearsed, who will be in the skits, approximate time that each skit rehearsal will run, order of rehearsals, and lunch and dinner breaks. There is no possibility for large miscalculation and it's almost frightening how accurate the mimeographed daily schedules are.

In addition to the six-day, in-office workload that is visible on these daily routine sheets, there is homework. This includes reading, writing, rewriting, memorizing lines, considering costumes and stage directions, and any other little details. The winner of the "Final Details" contest is Dan Aykroyd, who bubbles with requests for every kind of prop and costume before anyone else. Aykroyd is an incredibly driven person with intensity coming out of his ears. Even in the early read-throughs, while everyone is first

The *SNL* troupe work together like "Bees." Many of those extra actors are actually writers, prop men, and set designers for the show. (Edie Baskin/NBC)

Studio 8H has its own barber shop, makeup room, lounge, and a maze of other spaces that nearly create a closed community. (Dr. Steve Ryan)

hearing the lines, many of which will end up being changed or dropped, Aykroyd is concerned with his delivery and facial expressions. As *SNL* writer Michael O'Donoghue observes: "Most comedians or actors will try characters out on you from time to time to see if they work, but with Danny they just seem to leap out of nowhere. It's utterly startling because you think he can do anything: he can just make it up, fully realized, on the spot."

Near the stage area is a maze of rooms housing "departments" like makeup, barbers, snacks, lounge, dressing rooms, bathrooms, and utility spaces. In addition, the *SNL* crew maintains offices on the 17th floor, private spaces where they work out all those little details before letting them onto the stage and, finally, the tube. Each tiny office looks out on a general recreation room which should be put under glass in a museum. There are lots of toys: a ping pong table, a huge color television, a soda machine, and some electric video games. A child's garden of twentieth-century delights.

By ten o'clock, Wednesday's read-throughs are winding down into a series of meetings and conferences about tomorrow's schedule. There's a little more tension than usual for a Wednesday because the infamous Albanian, John Belushi, is still out in Hollywood and has not yet returned to New York.

On Thursday, the studio is different in feeling. Walter Matthau, the guest host, is buzzing around being fitted for his "Bad News Bees" costume. Writers are jockeying for position, trying to lay claim to various spaces in the studio to rehearse their skits. I walk over with one of the writers, Don Novello (who also plays

Everyone's favorite father, Guido Sarducci, is actually writer Don Novello, a key member of the double Emmy Award-winning staff. (NBC)

Father Guido Sarducci), and watch a skit he also co-wrote, which is called "Greek Restaurant." It's uncanny: Novello stands at the side taking notes, changing a few lines, making directorial moves, and *then* actually playing a bit part. It's funny to see all the writers running around because you recognize them instantly as all those extras who continually pop up in the skits. On this show, everyone gets into the act.

On Thursday the read-throughs mature to run-throughs, which means that the cast is expected to be familiar with the material at this point so that the cameras can follow them around the stage, gradually working up to the actual timing of the show. "Camera blocking," when the cameras get their angles and positions, is extremely critical for *SNL* because it is a live show, run at a breakneck pace. A few seconds lost on a camera move can mean the difference between the camera being at the right place for the next scene, or throwing the whole place into panic.

The skits are moving along and you begin to get a sense of what's actually going on. Again, the action is over at the "Greek Restaurant" as Don Pardo blares over the loudspeaker, "La-dies and Gen-tle-men . . . John Belushi!" The mad Albanian has just returned from Hollywood and he has a glazed look in his eye. "Here's a man," observes Aykroyd of Big John, "who jumped right out of a tank for Spielberg. [Aside] And damned near got killed!"

Now that Belushi is on the set, the pace quickens. The faint feeling that the show will not come together by Saturday is subsiding in a whirlwind of Belushi energy. "There is no show," emphasizes Lorne Michaels, "until the show." As the evening ticks on, every skit is rehearsed over and over. The only skits that are not rehearsed are not yet written; both the "Weekend Update" and the opening monologue scripts are actually written on Friday night so that the hottest "news" scoops can be included.

Davey Wilson, director of the show, is perhaps the friendliest man on earth. This helps to keep teamwork up, tempers down, and, ultimately, *Saturday Night Live!* running full speed ahead. He is largely the cause of the show's visible harmony, a point that is under-

John Belushi had a feverish final year on the show, commuting between Hollywood and New York. (Edie Baskin)

scored by the fact that for four years not one person in the entire production has called in sick.

By Friday, Studio 8H has been successfully transformed from a large, empty space into a framework of evolving sets: Nixon's study, Julia Child's kitchen, an Army surplus store, and a Greek restaurant complete

"Howd'ya like 'em?" shouts Cheeseburgahh King, Danny Aykroyd in "Greek Restaurant." (Edie Baskin)

with griddle. Aykroyd turns to the prop man and raises an eyebrow as he points at the gas griddle. "You sure this thing won't blow up?" Satisfied with the response, Danny strikes a match and immediately fires up the grill, an extra matchstick clamped in his jaw. "Howd'ya like 'em?" whispers Aykroyd to a cameraman, as Danny delivers a tray of cheeseburgers to the crew and the skit winds down.

At the other side of the studio, Gilda hugs a teddy bear waiting for the rehearsal of a piece called "Bedroom." Walter Matthau, this week's guest host, strolls onto the set complaining that he never gets the same limousine driver two days in a row. Bill Murray is mimicking Matthau's every syllable. Matthau sees this and starts cuddling Gilda, while insulting Murray. Bill, not the kind of guy who gets insulted too easily, lunges across the bed in fake anger, pushes his face right into Matthau's, and snarls, "Hey, back off, Pop. This ain't Hollywood, ya know." Everyone laughs.

At the other end of the studio, Dan Aykroyd is busy describing his new dress. Danny is rehearsing a skit he also wrote, "Julia Child's Kitchen." As in most of the pieces Dan writes, the action is fast, and funny. Also, something will probably die or be maimed. It could be a fish, as in his infamous "Bass-o-Matic," a couple of cows ("Mel's Hide Heaven") or bunny rabbits ("The Bunny Hut"),but something's gotta go. In this skit, it's Aykroyd himself, as he plays Julia Child, the gourmet chef. While making a cut to produce perfect chicken parts, Danny slices off his prop rubber thumb. But something isn't up to Aykroyd's standards.

The prop people come over to discuss the various methods of making blood shoot out of the fake thumb.

Guest host Walter Matthau, Bill, and Gilda in a skit called "Bedroom." (Edie Baskin)

The idea of a bag of blood in the thumb is mentioned. Danny shakes his head. "Nah. Not enough blood. There's got to be blood shooting out all over the place." The prop man and Aykroyd go over the various possibilities and suddenly you see Dan's eyes light up. "That sounds like the one." Dan winks as the prop crew scurries away with a design mission.

Saturday is D-Day. Set designers have been up all night Friday and the studio has been transformed into a tiny wonderland of make-believe places. Garrett Morris is decked out in a fitted black tux, and the morning begins with his singing a selection from a Mozart opera. Gilda Radner is walking around chewing bubble gum and hugging a teddy bear. She has a frantic look on her face. Suddenly she's pawing through her bag and furiously picking up coats off of the seats. Throwing her hands up in the air, she squeals with sad eyes, "Has anyone seen my keys?" Writer Alan Zweibel points out, "Yeah. Try around your neck." Sighing in relief, Gilda sees her keys dangling from the long chain she bought so she wouldn't lose them. With a heartfelt "thank you" and a little smile, Gilda dances away looking cute.

Costumes are still getting their final touches and Aykroyd is having his typical let's-get-this-perfect hard time as he adjusts his Julia Child wig. The new prop on his fake thumb is a long, rubber tubing that runs down his sleeve, out the bottom of his dress to a little pump filled with stage blood. As Danny screams "YyyYowwchH!! I've cut the dickens out of my finger!" the prop man activates a stream of blood that gets progressively larger. It begins as a noticeable

Playing Julia Child, Danny was a real cut up. (Edie Baskin)

trickle, increases to a steady flow, and ends up shooting cascades of blood into the air. Julia, or Danny, ends up dying in a pool of blood that could fill an average-sized tub. Aykroyd gestures with a "thumbs-up," announcing, "Hey, that thing works great." He turns to the video crew with yet another request: "Listen, I'd like to see that performance. Could you save that tape and let me go over it a few times?"

There is something unbearably funny about seeing John Belushi stuffed into a bee outfit. Here is a grown man, having important discussions with a group of people. Discussions that involve subjects like his career, Hollywood, records, money... the works. But these take place while large springs, capped by Ping-Pong balls, bounce in every direction. The side shows are as good as the skits.

Laraine Newman struts by, looking like a high-fashion model posing for *Vogue*. Her suede suit is so fitted you'd think she'd grown it on. Laraine moves over to the set where she's doing a talk show satire with Gilda called "Woman to Woman." Gilda is the hostess and Laraine plays Vanessa, the 87-pound, rich, seen-it-all, 17-year-old model turned movie star. As Newman giggles endlessly, Gilda gets increasingly more biting with her questions, eventually hitting,

A number of Laraine's roles have been based on a character she created, "Sherry of the Valley." (Edie Baskin)

"You know Vanessa, you must feel pretty bad knowing that you're just the kind of woman that other women love to hate." Vanessa simply rolls back in her chair, laughs evilly, and corrects, "Oh no. Not at all. You see, all my friends are young, thin, famous, rich, and successful, so we don't care what fat, old... *burp*!!" The first belch to ever register on the Richter Earthquake Scale. Gilda falls off her chair laughing, and everyone else is cracking up.

John Belushi is running around looking for some lost piece of his "Greek Restaurant" outfit. There it is: a black moustache. Perfect. Who'd ever think that a few hairs could be the thing to transform Albanian into Greek? Belushi is walking around, mumbling aloud. In a few minutes he'll be doing his first run-through of a "Weekend Update" spot on Christmas. It goes like this: the only thing John wanted for Christmas was a pony. He was so excited about it, he couldn't even sleep. He even had a name picked out and had even saved all of the food *he* could have eaten for his new pony. He woke up on Christmas morning with his pony ride all mapped out in his head but when he got downstairs and looked under the tree, he snarls, "Ya know what I got? A sweater. And it didn't fit. So I gave it to my brother, who I hate. And I hate Christmas. This year if I don't get a pony, I want a shotgun..." Aykroyd is watching the rehearsal very seriously. He observes: "That man is great. What a performance. Insane. Criminally insane." Danny has an extremely refined voice, deep and dignified. It is, however, in startling contrast to his bee outfit.

It's now 7 o'clock. In one hour the studio audience of about 300 people will sweep in and pass judgment.

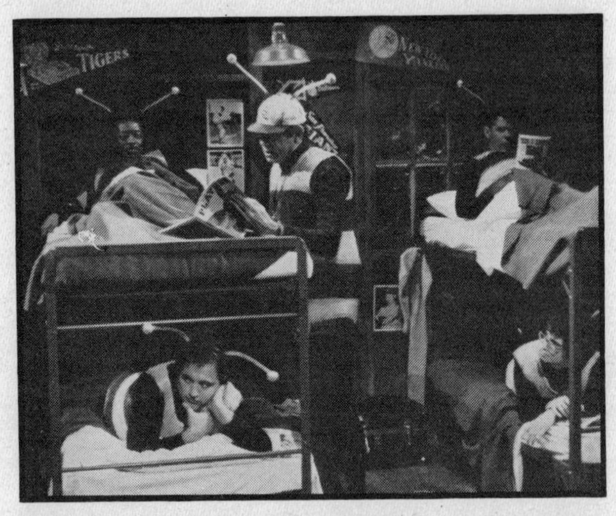

"The Killer Bees," like "The Coneheads," and several of Gilda's characters, have become *SNL* classics. (Edie Baskin)

At least two skits will be dropped. Everyone is scrambling for the final touch that will make the show whole. Wardrobe produces a pair of leg warmers for Danny, a last-minute detail for "Surplus Store." Jane Curtin is staring at the "Update" globe. This time, Gilda has lost her purse. For Bill Murray, things don't change. Pointing at a crew woman slumped in her seat, Murray calls out to the house, "Will somebody *please* poke that woman over there. I mean this ain't slumberland, ya know."

The cue card system is another of the unknown keys to the show's success. Al Siegel is in charge of the cue cards and he ends up with anywhere from 700 to 1,000 cards for each show. Each actor in a sketch gets a different color writing on the cue cards, with the guest

Al Siegel mans the "cue cards" for *SNL*. Each player gets a different color line in a sketch. (Edie Baskin)

host always getting black The cards themselves are white oaktag, as you would use for postermaking, and are around 30″ x 40″. "On a lot of shows you can just write the script and the changes are minimal," explains Siegel. "Here we make changes right up to and even on the air." The basic requirements for a cue card writer are neatness, extreme speed, and the ability to keep all the work in perfect order. Writers' cramp, and in Siegel's case colorful fingers, are part of the deal.

The dress rehearsal itself is more than a formality. Between the dress rehearsal and airtime there are approximately 90 minutes to make final changes. The studio audience passes judgment on the success of a week's work. Either they laugh or they don't. They will determine whether a skit is kept or dropped.

Bill Murray jumps out like a tiger, ready to "warm up" the crowd before the actual dress rehearsal begins. "How much did you guys pay to get in here?" asks Wild Bill. "It's free," screams a voice from the crowd. "Well, in theory, yeah," reasons Murray. "Well, look, I know I got $25 a pop for the tickets I sold to you guys and I'm just wondering what Belushi's getting. Now you don't have to tell me but I think I should know. Let's see a show of hands: Who paid more than 25 bucks to get in this place?" Everyone laughs. Bill's got the engine running and the show is beginning to "cook." The actors are visibly nervous but they are dying to get going.

By the time Walter Matthau meanders onto the stage, the audience is a pack of howling maniacs. Just as he planned. "I think of myself as a broad-minded, tolerant, even permissive man," begins Matthau in pointed seriousness. "But I have never been able to

Behind Garrett Morris's toothy smile and jive talk lies a real-life opera singer. Classically trained in musical composition, Morris is also an accomplished playwright. (Edie Baskin)

abide the kind of music usually played on this show. I prefer music to be tranquil, or else quietly stimulating, but rock and roll is to me an assault on the senses." Matthau goes on to explain that he demanded a quiet period of music, classical music, and introduces the famous tenor Paul McFerin Hayes to sing an aria from Mozart's *Don Giovanni*. The audience is dumbfounded. They are all looking at each other trying to figure out what gives. "Should I laugh?" is the question on everyone's faces.

Of course, Paul McFerin Hayes is Garrett Morris. It is a bit startling: a singer performing a Mozart aria on national television for an audience of 25 million people whose expectation was crazy comedy. And the audience, most of whom have probably never been to an opera, is clapping loudly.

You have to move quickly because you're right in the middle of the action. In a room off to the side, Danny Aykroyd is shooting the breeze with Art Garfunkel and Belushi is being advised by some record company "Biggie" that the Blues Brothers album is taking off even faster than The Rolling Stones. Gilda is surrounded by a bunch of sizzling Hollywood starlets who want to know if she will play Olive Oyl to Robin Williams' Popeye. As a team of makeup artists and hair designers create a world of characters, a show is going on just 15 feet away.

The writers watch over their skits like mother hens, furiously taking notes during the dress rehearsal. The speed is incredible. First they observe the skit, check the audience response, rework, reword, and revise. As the dress rehearsal ends, the entire cast makes a beeline for the offices. The atmosphere is a jumble of comments and gestures, rewritten lines and questions.

It's now 10:50, which means that the dress rehearsal ran nearly 20 minutes longer than the show will allow. The unfortunate nominees for "Not Enough Laughs" are Danny Aykroyd for his role in "Julia Child's Kitchen" and Danny, Jane, John, and Laraine for their participation in "Dormifix." As it turned out, Aykroyd revamped "J.C.'s Kitchen" and it was a winner when it was aired. "Dormifix," however, is buried in the television cemetery. Perhaps it is better there, anyway.

Nothing is sacred before the satirical eye of *SNL*—least of all, politicians. (Edie Baskin)

The studio audience is pouring in and, as always, there are thousands of people standing on line, each hoping to be one of the 300 admitted. The attempts that people have made to sneak into *SNL* have been just as creative, and probably more zany, than the skits on the show itself. The action is a little rowdy but, fortunately, no one has ever been hurt in the course of jockeying for position. Larry Gray, *SNL*'s publicity man, collects sneak-in stories. "In addition to the thousands of people who have tried to pose as 'press,' which isn't a very creative, nor successful method," explains Larry, "there have been a few good tries, some of which even worked. The best one was a girl who took the elevator up to the penthouse dining room, went to the ladies' room, snuck out the back, and actually walked down 57 flights of stairs into the studio. For the record, though, the usher caught her and she didn't get in."

The bugle is about to sound and, ready or not, the troops must answer the call. The show opens with John Belushi playing the part of Fred Silverman, NBC's president. John had fumbled through this particular scene in the rehearsal, complaining quite a bit about lines and mumbling about "cheap shots." But as irritating a guy as Belushi can be, one thing always is in his favor: You can always count on John to do his best when it counts. Only two days ago, Belushi practically crawled into this studio without a grip on the material, plus a seeming dislike for doing half of it. Now he's got half of America glad they stayed home to watch.

A keen eye will spot hundreds of changes on the cue cards, underscoring the ability of this crew to execute changes quickly. Whatever personal hassles anyone has are now buried under a thick layer of belly laughs. Right now the laughs are ringing all over America as Pat Nixon (Jane Curtin) is slamming Tricky Dick (Dan Aykroyd) with one joke after another.

It reaches a point where you are confident the show can't miss. The atmosphere changes from tension to relief to total party. As the final sketch ends, the cast gathers together for a little group bow and a wave good night. As has become the *SNL* tradition, a cast party is held at a Manhattan restaurant which is rented for the occasion. Gilda, Bill Murray, and Bill's brother, Brian, arrive first. Bill carries Gilda out onto the dance floor, performing the most exaggerated tango ever, while Gilda cries, "You're crazy. CRAZ-E. Let go!" Finally, Gilda is won over and she's dancing all over the floor. Jane, who doesn't like nightlife, and John and Danny never show up. Garrett Morris is holding court over at his table receiving congratulations. Garrett replies for the entire cast: "I'm glad you all liked it but it's no big thing. You know we're gonna do it all over again next week."

★ ★ ★ ★ ★ ★ ★ ★ ★ ★ ★ ★ ★ ★ ★ ★ ★ ★ ★

★ ★ ★ ★ ★ ★ ★ ★ ★ ★ ★ ★ ★ ★ ★ ★ ★ ★ ★

It's the Gilda Radner Show

She's so genuinely friendly and nice, Gilda Radner makes Gary Coleman look mean. And that's pretty hard to do. Despite all those varied and crazy characters she plays, she remembers warning Lorne Michaels four years ago that, "Every character I would do would be a nice Jewish girl from Detroit. But somehow, between writers, costumes, and makeup, other characters emerged. Roseann Roseannadanna came about from a wig that struck me so funny, I made up a whole world for it. Also, a major person in my family was this person who worked for us, Mrs. Gillies, who I called Dibby. I based Emily Litella on Dibby. I love Emily Litella, and I love to do it, I feel so comfortable. But I feel that I can do so much more. I found that the public being deluged with the 'never mind' thing is not my dream. When you go down the street and everyone's yelling 'Never mind, never mind,' you're going, 'Wait, I can do more than that.' I don't want to go to an early show business grave with 'never mind' around my neck."

"I don't want to go to an early show-business grave with 'never mind' around my neck. I can do more than that." (Edie Baskin)

Gilda remembers growing up as a fat kid who always liked to be funny. She attended an all-girl school and remembers: "You were better liked, not by who you were dating or if you were a cheerleader or what clothes you had, but if you were funny. At coeducational schools, a girl who was funny was frowned on by the boys. But for us it was *great,* an added asset. The years I went to college there were still curfews. I had new comedy material about the guys who didn't ask me out, to entertain the girls in the dorm. Recently my best girlfriend, Judy, who lives in Toronto, came to see me and said,'Boy, Gilda, it's real strange to see you making a living at what you did in my bedroom the whole time we were growing up.' "

Making a living is no longer one of Gilda's problems. Her Broadway show was such a success that the show's run was extended an extra two weeks to calm down mobs at the box office. She has a large apartment in New York's most exclusive apartment complex—a superstar, super-rich environment where people like John Lennon just blend in. She has turned down movie roles that have been offered, refusing millions of dollars. And unlike many other stars, she dresses to please herself and "only wears things that I love. I think a lot of times I don't match." Gilda glides by at a *SNL* rehearsal wearing a gray antique waistcoat; a pale green, collared shirt; tan sweater; purple socks; and brown shoes. She is drinking hot tea but, nonetheless, blowing huge, pink bubblegum bubbles. Coordinated, no, but very cute.

But being cute is something Gilda worries about. She has been cute since her days with Toronto's *Second City Television*; cute as the only female star in *The*

"Being a little girl is something that is very much alive in me." (Edie Baskin/NBC)

National Lampoon Show. And she is very cute on *Saturday Night Live*. At 5'6", 108 lbs., you know that deep down, Gilda *really* prefers being cute to being sexy. Maybe it *is* that since Gilda herself, says, "Being a little girl is something that is very much alive in me, and I sometimes get worried that my body will betray me on that level. I have a feeling that I'm getting too old to play Judy Miller." But her acting is so convincing, the audience feels very differently. One gets the feeling that Gilda's stage characters are such close approximations of her own life because she does not try to separate the two. She loves the show because "the fact that it's live makes it unusual and honest. Whether you see me as depressed or ecstatic, that's me. They tell you"—Gilda shrugs—"that you should keep a public personality and a mystique, but that wouldn't be me. I can't lie." But she often wishes that her public personality would be less visible. "In order to develop material, you can't always be onstage. You've got to be watching, too. If I can't go to a grocery store, and do my shopping and say to myself, 'Look at that lady over there, that's *really* weird,' because she's looking at me, then I've lost my school." But Gilda has figured a way to combat this: she's made her acting career her personal life: "I'm working with people I've been with for the last four years." *SNL* director Davey Wilson says, "What can you say about Gilda? She's just such a sweetheart that we all love her around here. She's a little kooky but she is just a joy, a pleasure to work with."

There is, however, one problem that Gilda created for the hand-held cameraman, Vince DePietro. "The first time that Gilda Radner did Roseann Roseannadanna on 'Weekend Update,' " remembers DiPietro, "it was the first time I had ever seen it. Now, normally I would have the camera focused on Jane or Murray. Jane introduces Roseann Roseannadanna and I pan [shift camera focus] over to her as she does her routine. This is the first time I've ever heard it and I'm cracking up so bad that the camera is shaking. Finally, Davey [*SNL* director] comes over and says, 'Hey, c'mon! Stop laughing, the camera is shaking.' I said,

'Dave, it's the first time I've heard it—let me get it out of my system. I won't laugh on the air.' But I *still* laughed on the air! Every time I hear her, it breaks me up."

Like other comedians, Gilda tends to apologize for not being funny off camera, but she really is. David Byrne of the Talking Heads remembers the cast party after they had been guests on the show. "The girl I was with has sort of kinky, Afro-ish hair. While we were sitting down, Gilda kept staring at us. Finally, Gilda came over, introduced herself, and says to the girl, "I *love* your hair, I really do. It's so, so...unusual. Can I rub my face in it?" And Gilda bends down and starts rubbing her face in this girl's hair! And she's making noises as she does it!" Byrne, usually a rather somber guy, is cracking up as he tells the story. Blinking his eyes to stop tears of laughter, he continues: "Gilda was great. Really just great. The party was pretty dull until she got started."

Althought Gilda is clearly the *female* star of the show, there is no jealousy among the other actresses. The women in the cast sit together at rehearsals and jabber away like three best friends in the school cafeteria. Gilda is quick to point out that they learn a lot from each other. "I learned from Laraine how to sustain a character. Jane taught me how to deal with the camera. She's got such wonderful diction and cool, you know? I used to jump out of the camera because I would get too excited. The girls—me, Jane, and Laraine — get along better than ever because we really depend on each other a lot. We've begun to work more as a repertory company. We've told each other about every dog we've ever had, every boyfriend, every bedroom and how it was decorated. And we've even begun to reminisce about our first year on *SNL*. It's real supportive. That's not always the case, of course, but it's nice."

Gilda, here interviewing The Fonz, is a perfect Baba Wawa. (Edie Baskin/NBC)

Gilda, more than any of the other performers, relates to the show as "a mom and dad and 20 kids huddled around the table. *Saturday Night Live* is great. It's theater, it's live. But, for me, it's also the family I missed with all the positives and negatives that that entails."

Gilda's own family is small; she has only one brother, and her father died when she was 14. "I was a fat kid growing up," recalls Gilda. "I adopted comedy as a way of life; it's my form of coping. My dad encouraged me a lot, pushed me out in front of people, sometimes to their distress. My mom was a tough audience, but if you got her to laugh, it was really great. I'd listen to her and my aunts discuss what a great storyteller their mother was and I'd think, 'Maybe something is passed on in your blood, something you're born to do.'"

Perhaps needing intimate encouragement is one reason Gilda is more interested in the theater than in movies. Radner's charm seems to peak at the sight of real people, a live audience. When asked about her future plans she says, "I know what I *don't* want to do. I don't want to do a situation comedy and I don't want to do movies. There's all that sitting around between takes—once I get started, it's pretty hard to stop me! Besides," reasons Gilda, fighting a grin, "I don't like to get up early." Joking aside, Gilda's attachment to live audiences is essential to her timing. When recording an album she actually *paid* to have a regular audience in the recording studio.

Bill Murray, Gilda's sometime boyfriend and Lisa Loopner's steady, says of Gilda, "She works harder than anyone on her lines. Gilda is an entertainer as opposed to a movie star or an actress' actress." All of a sudden he says, "Hey, did you hear about the fire in the baseball factory? Terrible, just terrible. Lots of people died because of all the balls on the floor." With that, Bill starts a balancing act as he trips away on imaginary balls. As entertainers go, these two are a pair.

And although Gilda has been receiving much praise, she remains a little insecure. Gilda Radner is always the first one to criticize Gilda Radner. "I love musicals, but I'm not a great singer. I can sing pretty loud, though." Asked about her interest in classical dramatic acting, she replies in her characteristic, down-to-earth way: "I have a sibilant 's.' I don't know if I'd be a good Lady Macbeth: 'Ith thith a dagger.' I'd be in trouble."

★ ★ ★ ★ ★ ★ ★ ★ ★ ★ ★ ★ ★ ★ ★ ★ ★ ★

Get Out of Here, It's Bill Murray!

It's Saturday night, around 8 o'clock, and the Blues Brothers are about to begin the dress rehearsal for *Saturday Night Live*. Usually one of the cast members or guests comes out before the dress rehearsal actually begins to 'warm up' the studio audience and Murray has assumed this function. So Murray bounds out onto the stage in overdrive, hip HIP! HURRAYING like the baseball coach that he was. Murray's job, as he sees it, is to "incite the fans," and he's clapping like a maniac as he calls for a show of hands. "How many of you out there are from out of town?" The hands go flying up, then Murray continues, "Good. GREAT. Now, how many of you are from New York? Can we hear some noise from the citizens of the Big Apple?" Again the hands go up, orchestrated by screams and maniacal cheering. Bill calmly gives a little clap, nods his head, and observes, "Very nice." A split second later, Murray grabs the microphone, jumps into the air and screams, "AWLL-RIGHT! Now whattaya say you locals beat up on ALL those OUT-OF-TOWNERS!!!!!" The place is going nuts, like at an Army-Navy football game, and the dress rehearsal, let alone the show, hasn't even begun yet.

"This man's a maniac, a MAY-NI-ACKKK, and I *mean* it." (Edie Baskin/NBC)

Murray is the more visible half of the only family act on the show: his brother, Brian Doyle Murray, is one of the writers. Like Radner, Belushi, and Aykroyd, Murray came to *SNL* from *Second City Television,* and it was his improvisational background that eventually led Lorne Michaels to switch Bill from the writing staff to the Not-Ready-For-Prime-Time Players.

A typical Bill Murray anecdote: After last year's opening show, Fred Silverman, NBC president, was walking down the hall to congratulate the cast when Murray grabbed him, knuckled his skull, and screamed something like, "Hey, you old maniac, get outta here. This man's a maniac, a MAY-NI-ACKKK, and I MEAN it." He means it.

With two starring roles in major films (*Meatballs* and *Where the Buffalo Roam*), Murray is already a big star with the potential to become, like Steve Martin and John Belushi, even bigger. Asked about the pressure of fans, he shrugs and says, "I sign autographs still, it's not too bad. I suppose if it got much worse I'd take the Robert Redford approach and just say I don't sign 'em. I can see how a lot of people think they're just silly. Hey, I'm not knocking it, I've gotten Ernie Banks' autograph myself. But the things I don't like are the 25 or more professional autograph people who wait downstairs every Saturday night. *Professionals* who take your autograph and sell it. I mean, really, what's your autograph worth?"

As Murray talks, he watches three television sets—two football games and a soccer match. Athletics is his passion. "The last few years, well, this friend of mine owns a minor league baseball team in Texas City, Texas, and I go down there as a sort of cheerleader. I'd take a little batting practice, coach first base, and incite the fans, which is what I did best." Murray's voice rises. "It was CR-RAZZY down there in Texas 'cause I really got to incite the fans A-LOT. . . ."

Murray's summer job was not, contrary to rumor, working in a Greek restaurant. What he did was coach baseball and incite the fans down in Texas. (Edie Baskin)

The *SNL* schedule is a pressure cooker and Bill helps let some of the steam off. Here's an example: Murray's on a set with Gilda and Walter Matthau, waiting for his cue. Like an athlete, an actor really has to get "psyched up" for his entrance, as if he were waiting for the gun at a track meet. At the signal, Bill fireballs onto the stage but WHOOPS!—technical problems. Matthau grumbles and Gilda whines, "Oh, NO! What's happening?" Bill dances around the stage singing, "Witchcraft. Wicked, OH Wick-ED Old Witchcraft..." Gilda and Walter look at each other and laugh. The skit starts rolling again when WHaaMM!! — sound problems short-circuit the rehearsal again. This time the delay is running long and each second clicks by louder than the last. Technicians are running around all over the place. Murray starts tapping his fingers on the desk, then slams his fist down and grabs the phone: "Operator, Lorne Michaels." Murray covers the receiver and announces to all, "*I'll* straighten this out!" A few seconds later, Bill is back on the phone. "Yeah, this is Bill. Listen, Lorne, we're down here working our tails off and I'm getting a little tired of this sweatshop, ya know? I mean, it's okay for you, MR. BIGMAN, up in his own quiet little office, while we go through hell down here. Now I've told you before but I'm not gonna say it again. If you think Bill Murray is gonna work like a dog only to have everything fall through because of cheap, broken-down equipment, you are WRONG my friend, uhn-uh. So you get down here right now and fix this stuff. BYE!!" And Bill slams that phone down. The entire crew is rolling in the aisles. Murray has been using a fake phone.

Murray likes to move fast and he is the most athletic of the Not-Ready-For-Prime-Time Players. "If I hadn't been a comedian or an actor or whatever it is that I am now," laughs Bill, "I would have been a professional athlete, probably a baseball player." If Chevy Chase's formula for great comedy — that it is "ultimately an athletic, musical thing" — has any validity, then Murray is in good shape.

The idea for Murray's infamous "Celebrity Corner," like so many of the *SNL* classics, was a joint endeavor. "I wanted to do, I don't know, show-biz stuff," remembers Murray, "and I had done the movie reviews before. Then Lorne asked me to do the news, but we didn't want to lose the movie reviews, so we just sort of combined the two ideas, called it 'Celebrity Corner,' and that's it. It's fun. It's fun because it sort of drags one more person into the action. It used to be just one person reading news jokes, then two people reading jokes. Now we sometimes have every person in the show on the 'Weekend Update,' and it's fun. Don [Novello] might do Father Guido Sarducci and Gilda, a Roseann Roseannadanna. Dan and Jane will do a Point/Counterpoint. I'll do my 'Celebrity Corner' with John or Garrett...so we're all in there. It takes it around and makes everything move a lot faster."

Bill had a hard time dealing with the breakneck schedule of the show during his first year as a writer. Now he's looser, acts, and often writes his own bits. (Edie Baskin)

Murray is probably the fastest developing of the *SNL* players. He's come a long way since his first year when "I didn't even know what I was doing, acting-wise. I tried to act and I tried to write and I tried this and that. I had a lot of trouble as a writer, getting things produced, and this is the whole thing, really. I wasn't used to these deadlines. I kinda say stuff like: 'I'll have it for you tomorrow.' But they'd say, 'TOMORROW!! This is too late.' Finally, toward the end of my first year, I did manage to write a couple of decent bits but it was hard for me.

"The next year, Lorne told me he didn't want me to write. And he told John [Belushi] the same thing because really we serve a better purpose if we work harder on the acting. And I actually ended up writing probably more when I wasn't a writer than the year I was because I did the movie reviews, most of which I wrote. And I ended up rewriting any I didn't write. But, really, anybody can write anything now and I like that. If I have a good idea, somebody else can take it and write it or we can write it together. Basically what I'm saying is that it's a cooperative effort and I work on everything just like everybody else. The writers do most of the writing and the actors do most of the acting but ... everybody does everything."

Murray excuses himself and takes his position on the stage. He walks to the front of the stage and scans the audience like an Indian scout. With a face of disgust, Bill points and whines, "Will somebody *please* poke that woman in the first row. She looks like she's gonna die, for Pete's sake." With that, Bill skips away, off into noogie heaven. And I really mean it.

★ ★ ★ ★ ★ ★ ★ ★ ★ ★ ★ ★ ★ ★ ★ ★ ★ ★ ★

Who Is Jane Curtin?

Jane Curtin is not your average mystery. She is seen on TV by millions of people every Saturday night, yet she rarely is seen offstage outside of her household. Jane, (alias Jane Face) is a good cook, an avid reader, and a woman who prefers quiet evenings by the fireside to champagne, limousines, and Studio 54. She will be friendly, even gracious to you. With her braided hair, she looks like Heidi. But Curtin, now that Howard Hughes has died, could well be America's least public public figure.

Jane Curtin was born on September 6, 1947, in Cambridge, Massachusetts, where her father runs an insurance agency and her mother is "a Radcliffe graduate who laments that she wanted to do something worthwhile but she had four kids instead." The Curtin four consists of brothers Jack, who works with Jane's father, and Larry, a stockbroker; sister Ginny, a teacher; and baby Jane, "the first one who ever moved out without getting married." Jane attended a series of parochial schools, then went to Elizabeth Seton Junior College and, finally, Northeastern University.

Jane did her first bit of acting in junior college and decided to try working in summer stock. One summer in Plattsburgh, New York, she met another aspiring actress, Amy Allen, who became a close friend. But they soon found themselves auditioning for the same role in a show being played at Harvard. Amy got the part and Jane recalls, "I decided I was going to cut my

Jane is a real-life beauty who avoids the public eye. (Edie Baskin/NBC)

fingernails and become a secretary and please my father. I give up easily and this was the first time I was turned down. But Amy talked me into auditioning for 'The Proposition.' "

"The Proposition" was a Boston-based improvisation group, and although Jane "had never seen it and had no idea what it was," her career was being formed. She fully expected to "audition for 'The Proposition,' be turned down, and get a job as an usher at the Charles [a Boston theater]. It turned out that I auditioned for six hours and was taken on that night. Of course, I didn't open my mouth for three months, and I hid behind people."

"The Proposition" was a big hit in Boston and also attracted quite a bit of attention when it came to New York in 1971. At the tender age of 24, Curtin had built up a following and was rapidly establishing herself as a star. Her mother was proud. But her father still felt that "it's a silly business and that I should work in the insurance company's death-claims department. Something steady."

New York is not a cheap place to live and Jane, despite her budding stardom, began looking around for work to supplement her "starving actress" level income. No, she did *not* take a job as a secretary. Blessed with long, silklike blonde hair, a striking face, and a picture-perfect smile, Jane was hired to perform in a toothpaste commercial. The pay was good but it wasn't exactly the highpoint of her acting career. "I sat for two and a half hours," recalls Jane, "saying: 'because of my high-brightening toothpaste.' How many ways can you say 'because of my high-brightening toothpaste'?"

With all the shuffles in the popular "Weekend Update," Curtin has remained the anchorwoman. (Rain Worthington)

Jane has incredible presence, that impeccable look of an organized professional. She exudes self-confidence. But nonetheless, she is sometimes very gullible. With childlike curiosity, Jane stands staring at the "Weekend Update" globe. Bill Murray watches intently, ready to pounce. He does the Murray stroll over toward Curtin, looking innocently available to answer questions.

"How do they make that globe spin?" asks Jane in total wonderment.

"Their hands, they, uhhh, spin it by hand," shrugs Murray, who quickly looks at the sky and winks at the audience, his head turned away from Jane. Is it possible that Jane Curtin, Ms. Intelligent Professional, will fall for this preposterous Murray lie? A lie told by Bill Murray, Noogie King, Goofball Extraordinaire? Shockingly, Jane bites with affirmative nod. "Ohh. I see."

Murray's eyes bug out of his head. "WITH THEIR HA-AAANNDSSS!! C'mon, Curtin. You mean, *you* fell for the old motor trick?" With that, Murray gives Jane a you'll-be-all-right pat on the back, and leaves Jane a very puzzled person.

Off camera, Jane is an avid hockey fan and met her husband, Patrick Lynch, at a Boston Bruins-New York Ranger hockey game. It was a blind date. For someone who seems so organized, this is a surprise. But then, nearly everything about Jane is a closely guarded secret, a blank spot in the gossip columns. When you have added up all you know about Jane, you find that she is invisible. Everything you wanted to know remains unknown. Everything you wanted to ask remains unanswered. Jane Curtin is no ordinary mystery. Perhaps when she chose her stage name, Curtin, she was trying to tell us something.

★ ★ ★ ★ ★ ★ ★ ★ ★ ★ ★ ★ ★ ★ ★ ★ ★ ★

Jes A Good Ole Girl . . . Laraine Newman

Whenever *SNL* needs a model, a beauty queen, or a love object, the writers always tap Laraine Newman. Maybe it's the way she carries herself or the way she dresses but, more likely, it's just the way Laraine is: an incurable romantic. "When I was a kid," smiles Laraine, "my favorite TV shows were *Zorro* because I was in love with Guy Williams, *The Man From U.N.C.L.E.* because I was in love with David McCallum, and *Mission Impossible* because I was in love with Martin Landau." When Laraine joined the cast, she had a crush on Danny Aykroyd. Her most embarrassing moment on the show was when she got caught by the TV camera "overkissing" Dan in a skit. Get the picture?

Like the rest of the cast, Laraine grew up on TV. She vividly remembers scenes from *Rocky & Bullwinkle,* who she "thought were very hip for a long time. Really great. They would do little things, like Natasha would be in disguise in Tijuana and her name would be Tequila Mockingbird. I didn't get it at the time but you see it later and you realize how wonderful it was." Laraine is filled with cartoon memories, Popeye and Bugs Bunny leading the parade.

Bearing in mind Newman's fondness for the tube, it's easy to understand why she would enjoy working on television despite her early interest in theater. Her

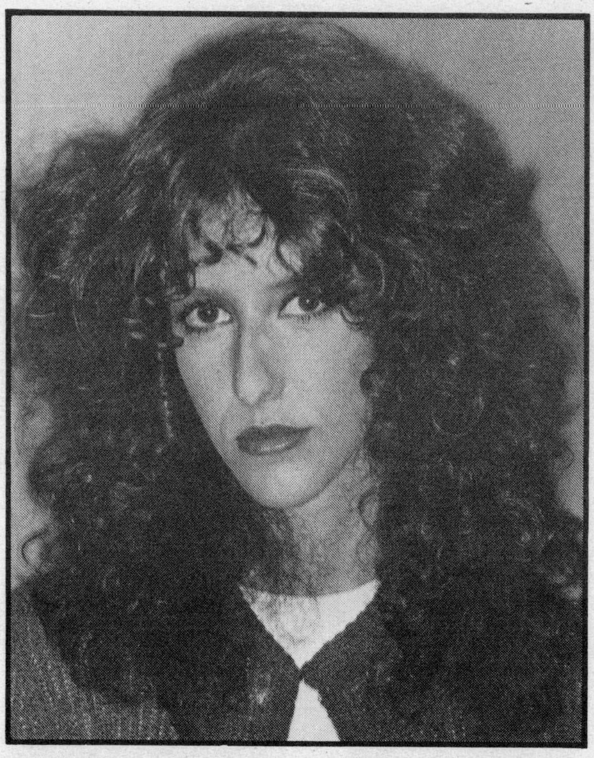

Laraine was initially interested in the theater, but she's a natural for television. (Edie Baskin/NBC)

first job as a paid performer came when Laraine was barely a teenager, starring in a Parks Department summer theater program in Los Angeles, where she grew up. But Laraine has come a long way since then. Her big break, the way she sees it, was her spot on *The Lily Tomlin Special,* which she calls "my first legit job." The Tomlin special was produced by Lorne Michaels in February, 1975, and Laraine was among the original group that came to New York in July of that year.

But getting the chance on the Tomlin special didn't just happen. Newman, along with her older sister, Tracy, and several members of an improvisation group called The Committee formed another troupe, called The Groundlings. They put on several performances in the Los Angeles area and soon had a strong local following. Local, but still in Los Angeles, which means a little something extra. Among the celebrities that attended various Groundling performances was Lily Tomlin. Laraine is quick to credit her sister, Tracy, who taught acting and improvisation. "Tracy was really responsible for encouraging me and helping me at critical times. I can't tell you how much, *really*; she helped me a lot."

"I had studied mime for four years," recalls Laraine. "I studied all through high school with a man named Richmond Shepherd. I was then offered the opportunity to study with Marcel Marceau [the great mime] in Paris. He took 100 students and it was a great thing to do at the time. I eventually stopped taking mime because I feel that mime gets very limiting after a while. But mime has opened me up in the sense that I know it so well that I don't even have to think about. It's part of me now."

Newman also studied ballet and jazz dance. But she quickly adds, "Mime is a discipline that I think would be more helpful to the performer than ballet or jazz dance. It broadens you in the sense that you learn to use gestures instead of relying on props. You discover your own gestures."

Laraine's off-camera life is at least as glamorous as her *SNL* creation, Vanessa, the 83-pound, 16-year-old, superstar, jet-set model. She is invariably the best dressed of the cast members, and everything about her seems dramatic or eye-catching. Her look is casual, but in an *ultra* fashionable way. She wears cowboy boots, but they are made of a very rich suede and have stitchwork patterns down the sides and around the toe. She wears corduroy jeans but the cut and fit are chic. Her hair is messy in a sleek way and the sweater is cashmere in a soft tan. Laraine is the epitome of California Cool. She can go to Studio 54 or ride a horse in the same outfit. And skinny, messy-haired or not, Newman is the kind of woman that makes guys turn their heads. She is not a natural beauty but is a fine example of how self-confidence simply makes one more appealing.

"The hardest part of doing *Saturday Night Live!*" winces Laraine, "is having a personal life. A personal life and a social life. We really work hard on that show and when we do it there's just no time for anything else." Laraine, who started with the show when she was 22, still loves to party. Her boyfriends have included rock stars and actors. But nonetheless,

"The top people in my field are Richard Pryor [shown here], Dan Aykroyd, and Albert Brooks." (Edie Baskin/NBC)

Laraine is always there to answer the call of *SNL*'s hectic schedule.

Laraine is also toying with the idea of becoming a writer, perhaps without performing. She is surprised that we're surprised. "I've written quite a few things for the show," shrugs Laraine, assuming this was common knowledge. "I wrote almost all my own material in The Groundlings and even some of that has surfaced with *Saturday Night Live*. Sherry, the girl from the Valley, is a character I did with The Groundlings. I wrote several other pieces for myself, as well. I'm writing a screenplay now, in fact. I would like to write more, I think. A lot of times I feel that maybe I don't like performing as much. It's not a natural part of me."

Laraine is very serious about comedy. "There are really just four kinds of humor," explains Newman analytically. "There's recognition, there's shock, there's silly, and there's violence." A versatile performer must be able to do all four, particularly now since comedy is becoming a big business, largely due to the success of her own show. "Now, more than ever," begins Laraine, "comedy has a real audience. A million improvisation groups are springing up around the country. It's a lucrative business now, so one could say that comedy does have the power, in the youth market at least, that rock 'n' roll had in the Sixties."

Although her offstage personality seems much like the roles she plays on the show, Laraine maintains that she doesn't plan it that way. "Most of the things I do on the show," insists Laraine, "are just written for me. I'm an actress and I accommodate the writers. I don't think they base their writing on the actors' personalities."

Laraine has been lucky enough to have the thrill of

working with some of her "heroes" on the show. "My favorite actor is Richard Pryor," beams Laraine. "Working with him on the show was one of the biggest moments of my life. To me, the top people in my field, those I respect the most, are Richard Pryor, Dan Aykroyd, and Albert Brooks."

Asked about her personal tastes in music, Laraine answers, "I like Elvis Costello, LTD, and Peter Gabriel." And while Lorne Michaels makes all the final decisions on guest musical acts, Laraine laughs when she explains, "We don't have any real say. But we can beg for our friends." One big reason why everyone enjoys working on the show, it's been said, is because they get to live out their dreams and meet and/or work with their idols. But Laraine will point out the real reason is that everyone feels absolutely secure and happy working for Lorne. It sounds very romantic.

★ ★ ★ ★ ★ ★ ★ ★ ★ ★ ★ ★ ★ ★ ★ ★ ★ ★ ★

A Berry, Berry Good Guy. . . Garrett Morris

"There's nothing really hard about doing the show," shrugs Garrett Morris, "because I love it and that makes it all cool. The worst part of the show, in a larger sense, is trying to get a wider range of roles not based on racial imagery. Obviously, I'm not the only one on the show who gets stereotyped—certainly Gilda and Laraine do. But I think that these stereotypes restrict *our*, and I mean *Saturday Night Live*'s ability to get the full spectrum of laughter."

Like Chevy Chase and Bill Murray, Garrett was originally hired by Lorne to write for the show. "I had written two plays," recalls Garrett, "one called *Stagger Lee* and one called *The Secret Place*. Lorne had read both of them and wanted to hire someone black so, I assume, he figured I had something to offer as a writer. Then he saw me act in *Cooley High* and decided to hire me as an actor. So, by the time the show began I was already acting. I did write quite a few things for the show at the beginning, as did Bill [Murray], Danny,

Garrett genuinely qualifies as a "high-brow" but he's a down-to-earth, nice guy. (NBC)

and John. But I don't think anybody in the Not-Ready-for-Prime-Time Players seriously wants to write because there's already enough pressure just trying to do the acting. It's ridiculous to make like Superman and try to do a lot of writing when we have a huge staff of writers who I think are very, very good. I mean, we still give suggestions and come up with things from time to time but, believe me, the acting is hard enough."

Garrett is the most classically trained of all the *SNL* players and he brings a whole different pitch to the show. Certainly it was a curve, maybe a screwball, to follow up the Blues Brothers with Garrett doing an aria from a Mozart opera. No one could believe that this was *Saturday Night Live*. Morris fields it all lightly: "I don't think it's any big deal, really. A man can be many things: a student, a carpenter, a baseball player, whatever. So it doesn't matter if I'm a comedian, an actor, a truckdriver, or an opera singer—and I can be all those things. It's no big deal, I'm still just Garrett Morris."

Morris's operatic training is the base of his musical background. He trained at the Tanglewood Music Festival, the Manhattan School of Music, and the Juilliard School for the Performing Arts, enough education to make him an unbearable snob. But quite the opposite. Garrett is the kind of guy who is most comfortable in tee shirts and bellbottom dungarees. Although he has "Cool" written all over his walk, wink, and joke style, Garrett is just a regular guy who grew up in New Orleans under the wing of his grandfather, a Baptist minister.

While nearly all the cast members of *SNL* except Jane Curtin are actively heading toward the movies, Morris is a confounding blend of diverse interests. He began his professional singing career as a little child who'd stand up on a table and sing gospel songs while his uncle preached. He continued in music for about 20 years, covering everything from conducting symphonies to composing jazz. Garrett landed a job as an arranger and singer for Harry Belafonte, then one of the most successful singers in the music business. National tours and appearances on key television shows were now in the cards for Garrett. After years of studies and struggles, the spotlight finally began to shine on Morris and he followed it directly to a new career!

"Music began to seem less free than being in a play," recalls Garrett. "In a play, you can use your whole body. Acting is more organic. It's you. Even now, when they ask me to sing, I feel uncomfortable unless I can approach it like an acting assignment. I don't know, with singing I began to feel like a court jester." Garrett got a part in the Broadway production of *Porgy & Bess*. His reputation as a "serious" actor grew by leaps and bounds as he continued to perform in Broadway hits. It was around this time that Garrett became interested in comedy.

"The roots of it probably go back to the Dixie Theatre in New Orleans," explains *SNL*'s sportscaster. "I'd go see Redd Foxx on Saturdays. Redd used to break me up! He *still* can do no wrong. I laugh as soon as he comes onstage. It's the way he does it that gets me. I mean, you take Don Rickles as an example. Not that I have anything against the man but he can be so cold sometimes. Foxx always did it with love and a feeling of sensitivity."

The show's elder statesman at 43, Garrett is ready to take yet another risk, publishing a magazine. "There's nothing definite yet," confides Garrett, "but I'm in the process of raising the money now. The working title is *Mahogany* and it will deal with all the issues vital to the black community."

Garrett, despite his comedic talents, is a serious man. He believes kids don't get enough on-the-level information from the mass media. He believes there is much hypocrisy in the world and would like to use his magazine to expose it.

Chico Escuela praying for rain. (Michael McKenzie)

Like Dan Aykroyd, Garrett has an acute interest in UFOs, mysticism, and other worlds. He practices Tantric Yoga and he looks in great shape at 5′7″, 150 pounds. He is an avid fan of Sherlock Holmes and whips both thumbs up when he tells you that, "I really dig my man, Sigmund Freud. Check out the dude's work. Old man Freud was into some pretty fine, detailed work. Not unlike Mr. Holmes in that respect."

He would also like to publish a book on the history of all the obscure black musicians who played all over this country during the 1940s and 50s. Garrett sees them as pioneers, like the players who were in the old black baseball leagues before Jackie Robinson was permitted to play in the majors. He maintains a strong sense of his heritage and is tireless at unearthing black history.

Although Garrett has a very serious side, he won't send us home without a laugh. "Maybe someday they'll be digging me up," reflects a pseudo-somber Morris. He turns from himself and becomes the gravedigger. " 'Oh yeah, Garrett Morris. I remember that guy. He used to be on *Saturday Night Live!*' "

★ ★ ★ ★ ★ ★ ★ ★ ★ ★ ★ ★ ★ ★ ★ ★ ★ ★ ★

AND SOME SPECIAL COUSINS...

★ ★ ★ ★ ★ ★ ★ ★ ★ ★ ★ ★ ★ ★ ★ ★ ★ ★ ★

I'm Chevy Chase... and You're Not

Chevy Chase is a non-stop charmer who is well aware of his power to put people on. "What I gave *Saturday Night Live*," offers Chevy matter-of-factly, "by hook or by crook, was somebody to bridge the gap between the reference points that the average American viewer is used to seeing on television and those found in troupes like Second City and National Lampoon. I look more preppie, more 'He looks like a responsible fellow, I guess I'll watch this show.' I was enough of a straight-looking guy to bridge the gap. I can charm my way through a dirty joke right in the President's face."

Chase is a wiry 6'4" ex-Bard College jock who started performing on TV largely because his best friend at college had his own video equipment. These early satirical skits surfaced as *Groove Tube*, which was shown at hundreds of colleges in "underground television" format prior to its distribution as a film. *Groove Tube*'s success probably was the deciding factor between Chase becoming an actor or a physician.

Chevy, giving a very Chevy-like smile. (Michael McKenzie)

Like former President Ford, Chevy was a jock...

but now he only trips for laughs. (Edie Baskin)

Chase, obviously, was the first cast member to achieve superstardom. Interestingly, when Chase first left the show and "headed for Hollywood" he called it "a cowtown. All you meet here are actors and people whose entire lives are dedicated to acting in an ad on television." At first he was very critical of the Hollywood "scene." Now, despite a few setbacks, he is less critical and more open-minded about his stardom and the Hollywood system. He says, "Imagine anybody in the world in any other profession, given the opportunity to make much more money and work at a higher level, not taking it because of some kind of crazy thing people would like to call integrity. What are we talking about here? Hollywood is really about the same as Times Square. When you are in New York doing underground shows or late-night television, it never occurs to you that maybe in ten years you'll be a big success and the people from all those shows will call you a 'sell out.' What it

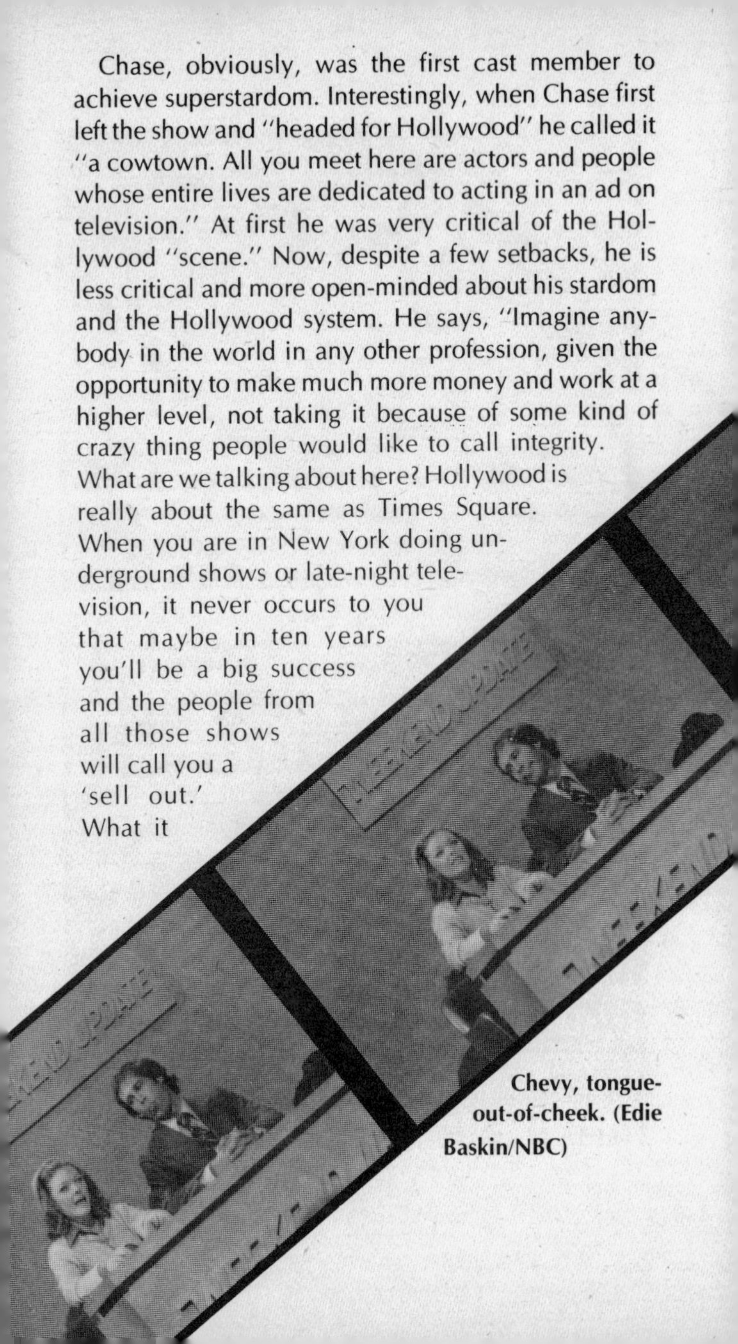

Chevy, tongue-out-of-cheek. (Edie Baskin/NBC)

means is that you become more visible and therefore open to more criticism, just as you are open to more praise."

Whether the members of *SNL* care to admit it or not, and they seem to disagree, Chase was responsible for contributing to the creation of the show. Among those features he helped create are "Weekend Update," a lot of the political satire, the opening of the show, and "The Killer Bees." But despite the criticism he has received for selling out, he denies any friction with his former cast members. "Actually," corrects Chevy, "there's a very close relationship. You really can't believe what you read, you know. Hopefully, you'll believe some of this, assuming I can continue to lie this well." That's Chevy, a charmer.

Chevy will take on an interesting acting assignment when he co-stars with the cuddly pup, Benji, in *Oh,*

Heavenly Dog! a film which will be released this summer. In the film, Chase is murdered, and in order to get into Heaven, he must first find his murderer. Unfortunately, or rather fortunately for us, the only available body in which he can return to Earth is that of a dog — Benji, himself. As you can imagine, a Chevy Chase–Benji team-up is something that's got to be hilarious.

★ ★ ★ ★ ★ ★ ★ ★ ★ ★ ★ ★ ★ ★ ★ ★ ★ ★

Steve Martin

"Yes, I'm a wild and craaaaazy guy!" screams Steve Martin as the audience goes wild. "The kinda guy who might do annnna-thiingg..at ANYtiime — to drink champagne at 3 A.M. or maybe at FOUR AAA.MMMM, or eat a live chipmunk or mayybeee even, maybeee EEE-VENN...WEAR *TWO* SOCKS ON *ONE* FOOT!" A lot like Chevy Chase, but more extreme, Martin is "that nice, respectable guy" who just kills you when he acts like a total maniac.

Although Martin literally burst onto the comedy scene with his appearances on *SNL,* he is a show-business veteran. At the age of five, his parents moved from Waco, Texas, to Inglenook, California, and Steve remembers that, "The first day I saw a movie, I knew that's what I wanted to do." Five years later, Martin's parents moved to Garden Grove, only two miles from Disneyland, and Steve got a job there selling guidebooks. He worked at Disneyland for the next eight years and learned rope tricks, magic, and how to make animals out of balloons. He also learned how to play the banjo and at age 18 he got his first acting job in

"YES, I'M A WIIILLLD & CRRR-AAA-ZY GUY!!!!!" (Atlantic Records)

a melodrama which performed four times a day at Knott's Berry Farm. Between each show, Martin would come out and do 10 minutes of craziness: music, magic, and jokes, which formed the foundation of his current act.

Somehow, Steve managed to get through high school "with B's and C's, though I was mostly a goof-off." He went on to various colleges with a major in philosophy, transferred to UCLA as a theater major, and worked in small clubs in L.A. perfecting his comedy act. His college career ended permanently when Steve, age 21, was hired as a writer for *The Smothers Brothers Show*. Although the show lasted only a short time, Martin picked up an Emmy as a writer and a string of writing jobs followed—for Pat Paulsen, Sonny & Cher, and Glen Campbell.

Like "King Tut," Steve Martin buys himself lots of gifts . . . a fur sink, an electric dog polisher, and some dumb stuff, too. (Edie Baskin)

Despite the large amount of money Martin was earning in 1973, he decided to leave L.A. He had had enough of the smog and the city, enough of the fast nightlife. Steve was dying to get up on the stage and perform his act again instead of writing bits for other people. So he jumped in his car and took off for Santa Fe. Then he cut his long hair and learned to ski. Finally, he donned a white suit and hit the road to try his luck on stage once more.

Martin had taken a big gamble, but it paid off. He had developed a hardcore following in local clubs and his first shot at national exposure (Oct. 23, 1976, on *SNL*) was a sensation. Since he "got small," Martin has gotten really big—his face has even peered out from national magazine covers. "I think it's good," reflects Steve, "that the joyful leaders of life, the entertainers, get the publicity instead of the murderers. Show business and gossip are interesting things—fun news. I think these are very optimistic times." With television, movies, and now a best-selling book (*Cruel Shoes*) to his credit, Martin can afford to be reclusive in his sprawling Aspen, Colorado, home. He is, in a word, rich. "I love money," gloats Steve. "I love everything about it. I've bought some pretty good stuff. Got me a $300 pair of socks, got a fur sink. Let's see, bought an electric dog polisher, a gasoline powered turtleneck sweater...and, of course, I bought some dumb stuff, too."

Martin doesn't let out much personal information. He drives a jeep, and likes to ski in the cool Colorado air. His hobbies are collecting American art, playing banjo, and listening to Irish folk music. But he's been very secretive for a particular reason. "The main

FOX-EZZ! (Edie Baskin)

thing," emphasizes Steve, "is that I don't want this information to distort my onstage character to the point that people can't believe it anymore."

Well, at least we know one thing about Steve: He's enormously talented and hilariously funny. What more could you want?

★ ★ ★ ★ ★ ★ ★ ★ ★ ★ ★ ★ ★ ★ ★ ★ ★ ★ ★

Ladies & Gentlemen . . . John Belushi!!!

Maybe you think that John Belushi is the type who has food fights in New York restaurants. Maybe you think he would sign an autograph to a little kid by asking, "What's your name, kid? Jimmy. All right kid, here." And Jimmy walks home with an autographed photo that reads, "Wise up, Jimmy, John Belushi." You might even think John likes to carry on, play pool, and listen to loud music. Well, you're right.

Born in Chicago on January 24, 1949, Belushi was a good student in high school, captained the football team, and also sang in the glee club. He studied for three years at the University of Illinois where he majored in drama, the source of his great Marlon Brando imitation. He also formed a comedy group at school and found a spiritual home when he discovered the Chicago branch of Second City Television. Belushi just couldn't believe that all the little skits he did, all the funny bits he'd act out for his friends and the funny pranks of his everyday life could add up to a close approximation of this important satirical troupe's kind of material. He quickly joined Second City.

Although Belushi has no great reverance for imitations, his "Duelling Brandos" is certainly tops. (Edie Baskin)

Belushi knew from the beginning what he wanted to do in show business. He also knew what he wouldn't do. "I couldn't stand acting in a lousy play," snarls John. "I like acting in my own stuff because I know it's good." Belushi is cocky but Belushi is good. Good enough to answer a casting call for "an actor who can play an instrument, do imitations of rock stars, improvise, and do comedy." This was the criteria the *National Lampoon* required to get a part in its Broadway show, *Lemmings*. "I can do *all* of that," shrugged Belushi, and Lampoon director, Tony Hendra, gave him the chance to prove it. Impressed, Hendra cast John as the show's announcer, explaining that, "I chose him because he projected the feeling of a homicidal maniac. Watching John act, you were always glad he hadn't taken up something more dangerous." The show was a huge success.

After *Lemmings* completed its run, Belushi got a spot with *The National Lampoon Radio Hour.* John wrote, acted, and eventually became Creative Director of the show, which was both a critical and popular success. Unfortunately, the show offended so many sponsors that it became impossible to keep it going. Undaunted, Belushi formed *The National Lampoon Show,* a long-running stage production in which he starred, wrote, and directed. Belushi then went all out to cement his Lampoon connection: he married one of the magazine's editors, Judy Jacklin.

When *The National Lampoon Show* closed in the summer of 1975, a revamped version of it was formed to tour the country. Belushi elected to stay in New York and, for the first time, he was an unemployed actor. As John looked around, he realized that at age 26 he had already been typecast in many director's eyes as an actor who could only do one thing: satirical comedy. "Because you're in a comedy revue, they think you can't act," snorted Belushi. "You're not *serious*. I did serious acting in college and in summer stock companies. I can do it. But nobody believes you." So it was partially panic that sent John to a television audition where he startled the producer by saying that he thought "all television was junk. My set at home is often covered with spit." This is not the kind of talk to get a job. Still, Lorne Michaels was too smart to ignore John's performance at the audition, a character Belushi called "The Samurai." HIRED!

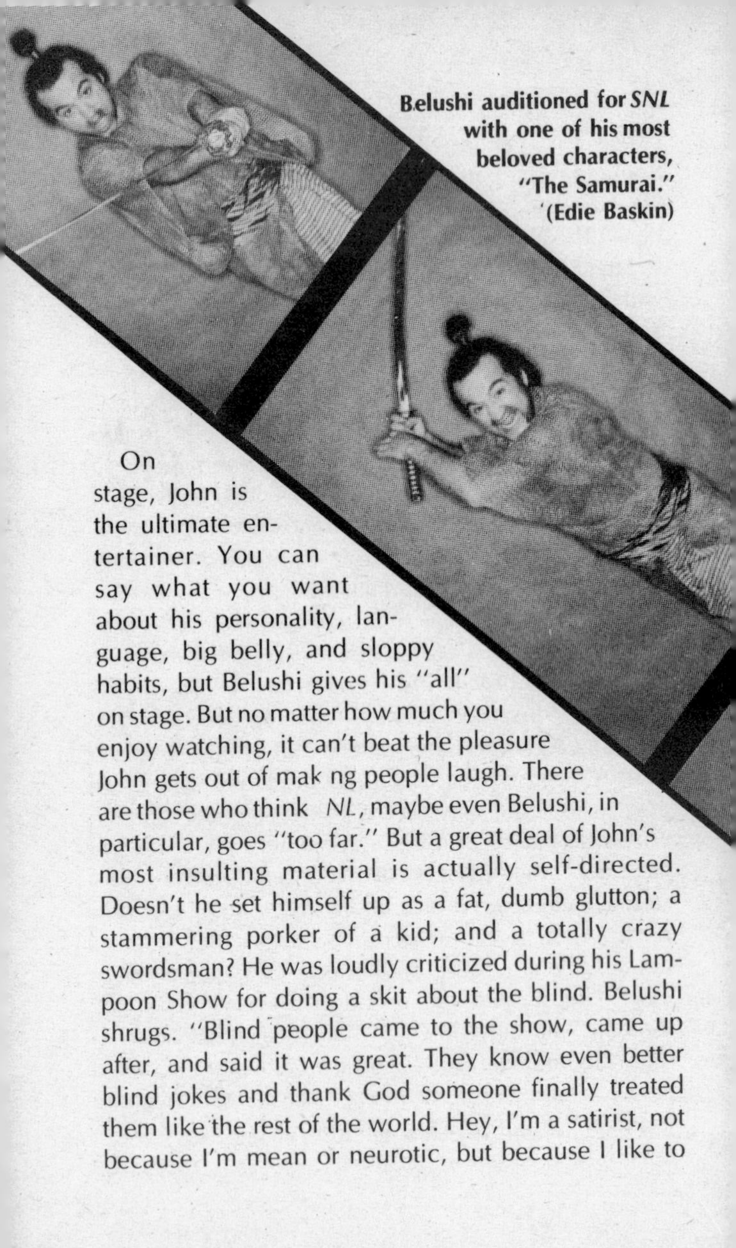

Belushi auditioned for *SNL* with one of his most beloved characters, "The Samurai." (Edie Baskin)

On stage, John is the ultimate entertainer. You can say what you want about his personality, language, big belly, and sloppy habits, but Belushi gives his "all" on stage. But no matter how much you enjoy watching, it can't beat the pleasure John gets out of mak ng people laugh. There are those who think *NL*, maybe even Belushi, in particular, goes "too far." But a great deal of John's most insulting material is actually self-directed. Doesn't he set himself up as a fat, dumb glutton; a stammering porker of a kid; and a totally crazy swordsman? He was loudly criticized during his Lampoon Show for doing a skit about the blind. Belushi shrugs. "Blind people came to the show, came up after, and said it was great. They know even better blind jokes and thank God someone finally treated them like the rest of the world. Hey, I'm a satirist, not because I'm mean or neurotic, but because I like to make people laugh."

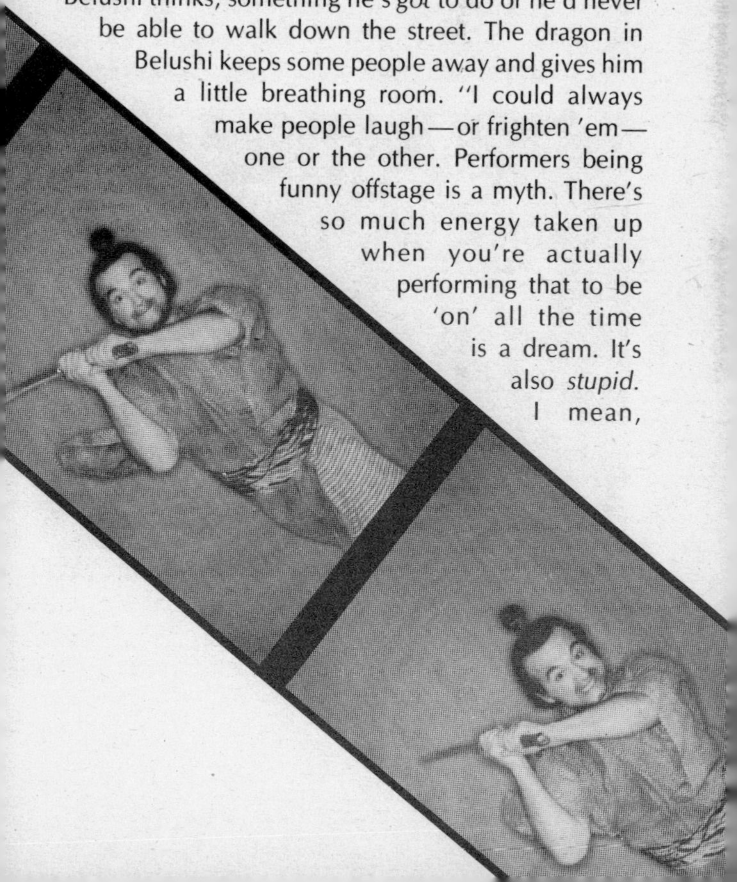

In public Belushi has a terrifying way of dealing with people. It's very easy to think he's a monster and you always have the impression he's about to break open your face. *SNL* director Davey Wilson says, "You know, it's easy to get the wrong impression of John. John's facade is that of a bullish, tough guy. But deep inside, John's a sweet guy, really. He's *always* working." This tough-guy facade has left more than one aspiring journalist shaking after dealing with Big Bad John. It is the price of fame, though, Belushi thinks, something he's *got* to do or he'd never be able to walk down the street. The dragon in Belushi keeps some people away and gives him a little breathing room. "I could always make people laugh—or frighten 'em—one or the other. Performers being funny offstage is a myth. There's so much energy taken up when you're actually performing that to be 'on' all the time is a dream. It's also *stupid*. I mean, when I'm with my friends and stuff, it's different. But when I talk to other people. I just don't even try to come up with one-liners."

As *SNL* colleague Michael O'Donoghue explained, "John has really become a solid professional which, for me, means that he continually went out there and delivered from eleven-thirty to one on Saturday nights. There are times that you sent him out there with almost nothing [no written material] and he'd make it work." But, there are times when it works and times when it doesn't. "Some things we've done have been dumb," shrugs Belushi. "We've done a lot of shows, you know, so everything isn't really a gem, a jewel of comedy.

"Call it stage presence or charisma or whatever"—Belushi's got it, explains a director. In every performance, he stands out. (Edie Baskin/NBC)

You just hope that you do one thing a week that's really good."

Belushi says he had a good time working with Elliot Gould, Buck Henry, and Steve Martin. "They're easygoing guys. They're not afraid to make fools out of themselves. They go out there and have a good time, which is the whole point of this show, right? But hosts who sit around and say, 'I'm a *big movie star,* I don't need this.' Well, we don't need *that.*" John pushes back his hat and continues. "Some people aren't as much fun to work with, but they're great performers and that cancels out everything. If you do a good show, you may be a creep all week but you're a fabulous guy in my book." When asked who he might like to see host the show, the ex-football player says, "I like sports. I'm a Bears' fan. I think Walter Payton [the Bears' star halfback] should get the Entertainer of the Year Award. I'd love to have him in the show!"

From the beginning of his acting career, Belushi managed to stand out in every production. Bernie Sahlins, Belushi's first professional director at Second City, remembers, "He was funny, he had a wonderful sense of timing, and he was a good actor. He played with better actors, but they didn't have what he had. The minute he hit the stage during his audition, I knew. He had the ability to get all eyes focused on him. Call it stage presence or charisma or whatever. It has to do with being totally *in* the moment—the ability to focus right there, right then. If even a small part of you says, 'How are they liking me?' or 'What am I doing here?' it shows. John had *none* of that. I even remember his first performance. He did a Shakespeare satire scene and he was *off*! John was an immediate crowd pleaser. His focus is so intense."

Intensity also helped John become an All-State middle linebacker who his football coach remembers as "a tough kid who loved to hit."

"I don't *ever* see John becoming that stable," continues O'Donoghue. "He is 100% Albanian, you know, the only one you're ever likely to meet. I tell him that Albanians are gypsies whose wagons broke down. I have this vision of him with a goose under his arm, trying to sneak out of the room. Yes," pronounces O'Donoghue, "that *is* John: an Albanian goose thief."

John Belushi is now a household name. His success seems more the coincidence that he loves to make

"I've gone to see *Animal House* five or six times. I'll wait until it's started, then I'll sneak in the back." Here's John with Linda Ronstadt. (Edie Baskin)

people laugh and we love to laugh at him than the product of something like ambition. For all the goodies fame has brought Belushi, it's also saddled him with his career's most perplexing problem. On the one hand are the fans screaming for all those great characters we love to see. But on the other hand is Belushi's own desire to explore new territory. "You've got to leave characters behind," emphasizes John, "take chances. I could do the Bees, or the Samurai, or Joe Cocker forever. I could do them in Las Vegas and make a lot of money doing it. But I made the decision early on to keep doing something new."

But John has to admit one exception to his own rule of never looking back. "I've gone to see *Animal House* five or six times. I'll wait until it's started, then I'll sneak in the back of the theater and watch it with a real audience. And when they laugh, it just makes me feel sooo good." And that tells you a lot: Belushi just wants to make us laugh, and we're happy to oblige.

★ ★ ★ ★ ★ ★ ★ ★ ★ ★ ★ ★ ★ ★ ★ ★ ★ ★ ★

Dan Aykroyd

The key to understanding Danny Aykroyd's personality is that it isn't just *one* personality but more closely resembles a comedy team, a whole group of guys out to have some laughs. "My parents have a photo of Dan when he was about three," remembers Danny's kid brother, Peter, who followed Big D to *SNL* as a writer and performer. "In the picture Dan is riding a small motorcycle, carrying a machine gun, and wearing a cowboy hat. In other words, even then he had at least three different personalities going at once."

Born in Ottawa, Ontario, Canada, on July 1, 1952, Daniel Edward Aykroyd is the son of Samuel Cuthbert Peter Hugh Aykroyd, whose Canadian government career presently carries the title of Assistant Deputy Minister of Transport for Research and Development. Danny began a normal life by entering, and then getting kicked out of, St. Pius X Minor Preparatory Seminary in Ontario. Aykroyd then pulled himself together and graduated from a co-ed high school. He was then graduated from Carleton University, majoring in criminology. He even went so far as to "work for the penitentiary service and write a thick manual on personnel placement for the Solicitor General's facility in Ottawa." In other words, he began a regular job and career. But Dan's eye was always on show business, even when he was in school.

By his junior year in high school, Danny's class clowning had taken on a more serious aspect. He began by starting rock bands and eventually acting for the comedy troupe, Second City Television. Aykroyd's band, The Downtowners, developed quite a local reputation and Danny was pretty much a hometown celebrity while still in high school. It was his association with the Second City comedy troupe that finally got him to New York.

Man of a thousand faces, Danny Aykroyd plays talk-show host, Tom Snyder. The gentleman playing Jagger is Mick. (Edie Baskin)

All of the stories one hears about Aykroyd can be broken down into two main categories: 1. those that are mostly true and, 2. those that aren't true at all. For example, it is true that Aykroyd's father, a candidate for World's Straightest Father, gave him an electric lawnmower as a gift. It is also true that Dan has had a number of part-time jobs from the age of 12, which have included: brakeman on a railway, warehouseman, dial reader on a runway load-testing unit ("I almost got killed one night at Toronto airport," claims Aykroyd, "when a DC-8 took off and grazed the station wagon I was riding out to the site in. Man, it was heavy"), and truck driver for the Royal Mail.

After about a decade of part-time jobs, Aykroyd and his buddy, Marc O'Hara, settled on a job they both knew they could handle: running an underground nightclub in Toronto called the Club 505. Danny calls it "the best joint that there ever was in Canada." It was the money that Aykroyd made from the 505 that allowed him to adopt such an "I don't care" attitude toward working on Saturday Night. "I'd work at Second City at night and run the club from one A.M. on," reveals Aykroyd. "The Club 505 was completely furnished with old Forties-style couches and armchairs, and a barber's chair, all scavenged and scrounged. We slept in lofts above whatever crept on the floor at night. It bordered on serious squalor at times. Life was comfortable."

Aykroyd waltzes into the *SNL* rehearsal, 6 feet, 180 lbs. of meticulously unshaven bulk. Dressed in a black Western shirt, loosened white tie, dark green corduroy jeans with one of those turquoise Cowboy buckles, and heavy motorcycle boots, Aykroyd still looks like the "three-character-at-a-time-minimum" multiple personality that he established as a child. Accept no less.

Aykroyd gives one of his famous Nixon imitations. (Edie Baskin)

Danny's office is a portrait of the inhabitant: something between a far-out three-dimensional spaceship and the prop room from a war movie. Davey Wilson, *SNL*'s director, observes: "Danny loves hardware, equipment: an old rifle, a cartridge belt... We did a sketch called 'Metal Detector' where we had a guy going through one of those airline security things and Danny went out and shopped—and I mean *shopped*—on his own. He went to one of those places on the

Bowery and came back with every bolt, plate, and piece of metal he could find. Danny's office is surrounded with model plane kits and miniature tanks and crazy things like early radio tubes. He's *into*," pronounces Wilson with a definitive headshake, "hardware."

It's Thursday afternoon, the first day of *SNL* rehearsals, and I'm standing near the stage, taking notes. Suddenly Aykroyd angles toward me like a curious tiger: "Hey," asks Danny, pointing at my collar, "where'd ya get the button?" I look down at my Blues Brothers pin, smile, and say, "From the press department. In fact, I just saw a whole shipment of them arrive marked 'DAN AYKROYD' and . . ." Aykroyd's eyes roll in his head, sure he's been robbed, as he screams, *"Where is that weasel!!!!* Did anybody here see Larry Gray?" But what I didn't tell Danny was that Larry did him a favor by signing for the shipment. Otherwise the messenger would have just taken them back. So I try to get through. "Hey, Danny," I correct, "Larry just signed for the buttons 'cause you weren't around . . .'" Aykroyd is finger-pointing, angry at this point, and interrupts angrier than before: "You're darn right I wasn't around! Hey, it's just like these sleazy press people, but he won't succeed this time. I'll have my secretary track that guy down. And thanks"—Dan winks as he angles toward his set—"for the tip." I head back to the Press Office to see what hornet's nest I've stuck my nose into. Larry Gray, the man in charge, takes it all casually and assures me, "Don't worry about it, Danny's like that."

Aykroyd really is like that—a nonstop stickler whose concern for minute detail is as much the source of his humor as it is the source of his abrasiveness. Both of these qualities are constants in Aykroyd's behavior. To give you an idea, this next incident happened only five minutes later. Aykroyd is playing the part of Nixon and the studio is ringing with laughter as Dan is scoring laughs with line after line, gesture after gesture. Aykroyd waddles, Nixon-style, over to his desk and begins to type a letter to the taxpayers when WHaaAAMMM!!! Danny slams the typewriter with his fists and screams, "This *thing* doesn't work." Al Franken, one of the writers on the skit, controls his initial impulse to beat Aykroyd to a pulp and makes the foolish mistake of trying diplomacy. "Dan, it's only a makeshift prop. We ... " Aykroyd shoves the machine across the desk. "Props are important. This thing has got to work. How do you expect me to type a letter?" Franken has obviously been down this road before and soothingly continues, "Don't worry, Dan, we'll get one that works. *Believe* me, we'll have it before Saturday." Danny hasn't even heard Franken and continues his complaint: "You can't imagine how this throws my performance." Franken remains sympathetic. "No, you're right, Dan." But big Dan goes right on, "...and it's got to be electric, maybe an IBM with one of those little balls on it. Is there an electrical outlet around here somewhere? Even the patience of a saint would have been worn thin by now, and Franken finally lets fly: "Dan, Do *not worry*, okay? I am quite sure that the NBC prop department is capable of turning up an electric typewriter. And if they can't, I'll bring mine—you can have mine! Now can we *please* continue?" Aykroyd now feels he'll get the machine but continues the electrical outlet argument. A stickler.

Conceived, written, and played by Aykroyd, the "Bass-o-Matic" sketch is Danny's all-time favorite. (Edie Baskin/NBC)

Someone once said, "You can't judge a book by its cover." Not true. You look at Aykroyd in his motorcycle boots and black shirt, then think about the parts he plays, especially the ones he writes: "Moth Masher," "Mel's Hide Heaven" (where you select your own cow at Mel's indoor, air-conditioned cattle range),

Irwin Mainway and the "Super Bass-o-Matic" which lets you "blend an *entire* bass to the thickness you desire." The "Bass-o-Matic" skit is Aykroyd's all-time favorite. The guy is totally fascinating.

It is no surprise, in view of Danny's Beldar Cone-head, that Aykroyd is interested in UFOs, psychic phenomenon, and the occult. "When Danny and I drive cross-country," explains John Belushi, "we always look for UFOs. I've gone up to his dead grandpa's farmhouse with him to wait for his ghost. Danny said he had seen him before and I believe him. He said it started as a green glow."

Meanwhile, back at the rehearsal, Dan is being difficult again. Writer Alan Zweibel has come up with a skit, "The Bad News Bees," that has the entire cast and crew cracking up at the rehearsals. Over 60 people laughing their heads off. But one guy is complaining about the script. Says Danny, "I can't say that, Alan. I mean, I'll feel ridiculous if I say that." Davey Wilson, the director, finally convinces Danny that he should deliver the lines at dress rehearsal and, if the audience doesn't laugh, the lines will be pulled before show-time. Aykroyd agrees, finishes the skit, and heads for his dressing room. "Hey, Danny," I intercept, "I understand you've enlisted in the Army." Aykroyd breaks into a grin. "Yeah, Steven Spielberg's Army [in the movie *1941*]. I play the part of a Motor Sergeant, Acting Tank Crew Commander. Machine guns and big bikes, VVvrrooo, vrrrooo, vvvrrrooommm." And Danny roars off on a dream Harley-Davidson into an imaginary sunset.

★ ★ ★ ★ ★ ★ ★ ★ ★ ★ ★ ★ ★ ★ ★ ★ ★ ★

It's The Franken & Davis Show!!!!

"When I come into a room they always say, 'Here come the guys,' even when I'm alone."

—Al Franken on F&D

The 17th floor office of Franken & Davis at NBC is a picture in itself: scattered yellow pads, hordes of ballpoint pens, a change of clothes, and a wall of video cassettes. Over this reigns a gold-painted plaster of Paris *official* Seal of Minnesota. The inner side of the office door has a bunch of handy, handmade signs that F&D tape to the outside of the door at critical times. These will advise the visitor to "Go Away" or inform, "Am sleeping on floor behind desk—not dead." The signs, like most of their writing since high school, are joint efforts. As well, they have done stand-up comedy on both coasts, Reno, Nevada, and, naturally, in their home state, Minnesota. They managed to keep the duo intact even while Al Franken, the short guy, studied Social Sciences at Harvard, as tall Tom Davis hitch-hiked, washed dishes, went to rock concerts, and

Huck Finned for four years. Neither seems to have lost the important thing: a sense of humor.

Franken and Davis polishing up their material. (Michael McKenzie)

How did the writers get hired for *SNL*? "We flew out here for the show on July 8, 1975," recalls Davis. "I remember the date exactly because I had tickets to see the Rolling Stones. The concert was *two days away* when we got the call to come to New York. I was questioning because we really didn't know what the show was about. We were hired without even being told what the show was. We gave some material to an agent, Herb Karp at William Morris, assuming, of course, that nothing would happen. He gave it to

Lorne, Lorne read it, liked it, and hired us. It's called 'being in the right place at the right time and *not* worrying about it.' It makes you wonder how many people turned down the job because they weren't told what it was before they were hired. Turning down *SNL*: now that's the kind of thing that can make a guy feel *real* bad.

F&D, or Al & Tom, are walking monuments to the "two heads are better than one" theory. They are largely responsible for many of the better Carter, Ford, and Nixon skits on the show, as well as staples like "The Bees" and "The Coneheads." In fact, Davis remembers being on Easter Island when he and Danny Aykroyd thought of those high-domed creatures from Remulak. They also came up with Theodoric of York, the Medieval Barber (who cuts off ears, leeches the blood, and squelches complaints with, "Hey, who's the barber around here?"), and all his medieval friends. Sick, funny, crazy, dry, heavy, and black are just a few of the words people use to describe F&D's humor. This show is a perfect outlet for their work and it's difficult to imagine what they would have done if they hadn't accepted a job from an anonymous television show. "We would have beaten Lorne in getting everyone together," answers Franken with an "obviously" tone of voice. "Right," nods Davis, "we would have invested in *Star Wars* at an early stage." "And," concludes Franken, "I would have written *Star Wars*."

There is no way of explaining the team-writing concept of F&D. The best thing is to give you a slice of a typical, unretouched F&D conversation. Despite the fact that Davis says they don't think of themselves as being hard-core cutups once removed from the show,

Our friends from Remulak, "The Coneheads," were conceived by Tom Davis and Dan Aykroyd. (Edie Baskin)

and they do have *some* serious moments, I'll let you decide. Remember, this is a real conversation. F&D talking to you.

Davis: I saved my own life once. You know those hand warmers, I mean hand *dryers* in gas station bathrooms? Well, it was *real cold.*

Franken: (*laughs*) I almost froze in a car, remember that?

Davis: Oh, yeah! We were doing a gig in northern Minnesota and we drove up at night. (*surprised*) We made gr-reat time. So we pull up in front of the high school at three in the morning...

Franken: (*correcting*) It was a college.

Davis: (*nods*) Right...in my Volkswagen Van. Damn, it was 30 *be-looww.* We had to wait until the school opened, right? And they had these big, cavernous showers which weren't exactly warm yet...

Franken: (*shivvvers*) Ohh, that was cold. Cold has a lot to do with comedy.

Davis: So the message is, to do comedy, SUFFER.

Franken: ...and buy some sweaters.

Davis: And some Chiclets.

Davis then procedes to bring out a large styrofoam box. In it is the coveted Emmy award, which both Franken & Davis have won *three consecutive years* now. Davis maintains his most recent Emmy is this hideous, *unopened* tomb of a case, shrugging, "Oh, I have the curiousity to open it but I also have the restraint not to." Meanwhile, Franken is explaining the funniest skit F&D ever penned, which the censors buried. "It's a David Susskind show, a theme show. It's, uhh, people who, uhhhmm, wanted to kill Ted Kennedy who are the guests. The first guy is asked why he wants to kill Ted and he says, 'You will know me and this *will* happen.' Franken is struggling to maintain a straight face when Davis picks up with, "Yeah, his name is something like Ray Weese, uhhm... he lives over a muffler shop and he collects pornography." Everyone in the room is laughing hysterically. Franken calms down. "We felt it was an important sketch which pointed out that these enormous tragedies are caused by *craz*-ies!" Davis is nodding agreement.

F&D on censorship: "You win some, you lose some." (Michael McKenzie)

"We weren't saying, in fact, that Ted Kennedy should be shot. Certainly there's nothing funny in that. But what is funny is how these things are perpetrated, what kinds of personalities are involved."

The ongoing Battle Of Censorship Point is, perhaps, the trickiest problem the show faces. Some of the best skits the show could have done, we may never see. How do F&D feel about being shot down from time to time? Franken shrugs. "We sign a contract with NBC saying they have this right. And that's the ballgame." Davis leans back in his chair like a philosophical football coach.

"Yeah," smiles Tom, "you win some, you lose some."

★ ★ ★ ★ ★ ★ ★ ★ ★ ★ ★ ★ ★ ★ ★ ★ ★ ★

SNL CHRONOLOGY

★ ★ ★ ★ ★ ★ ★ ★ ★ ★ ★ ★ ★ ★ ★ ★ ★ ★

Show#, Date	***List of Hosts***	***Guests Artists***
1975		
1. 10/11	George Carlin	Janis Ian / Billy Preston / Valery Bromfeld / Andy Kaufman
2. 10/18	Paul Simon / Connie Hawkins / Marv Albert	Randy Newman / Art Garfunkel / Phoebe Snow / The Jesse Dixon Singers
3. 10/25	Rob Reiner	Penny Marshall / The Lockers / The Nuns / Andy Kaufman
4. 11/8	Candice Bergen	Esther Phillips / Andy Kaufman
5. 11/15	Robert Klein	ABBA / Loudon Wainwright, III
6. 11/22	Lily Tomlin	Howard Shore & His All Nurse Band
7. 12/13	Richard Pryor	Gil-Scott Heron / Thalmus Rasulala / Annazette Chase / Shelley Pryor
8. 12/20	Candice Bergen	Martha Reeves/The Stylistics/ Maggie Kuhn
1976		
9. 1/10	Elliot Gould	Anne Murray / Franken & Davis
10. 1/17	Buck Henry	Bill Withers / Toni Basil
11. 1/24	Peter Cook & Dudley Moore	Neil Sedaka
12. 1/31	Dick Cavett	Jimmy Cliff / Alan Peterson / Marshall Efron

Gilda introduces guest host Elliot Gould to her "mother." (Edie Baskin)

Show#, Date	*List of Hosts*	*Guest Artists*
13. 2/14	Peter Boyle	Al Jarreau / The Shapiro Sisters
14. 2/21	Desi Arnaz, Sr.	Desi Arnaz, Jr.
15. 2/28	Jill Clayburgh	Leon Redbone / U.S. Coast Guard Choir / Andy Kaufman
16. 3/13	Tony Perkins	Betty Carter
17. 4/17	Ron Nessen	Patti Smith / Billy Crystal
18. 4/24	Raquel Welch	Phoebe Snow/John Sebastian
19. 5/8	Madeleine Kahn	Carly Simon
20. 5/15	Dyan Cannon	Leon & Mary Russell

Show#, Date	*List of Hosts*	*Guest Artists*
21. 5/22	Buck Henry	Gordon Lightfoot
22. 5/29	Elliot Gould	Leon Redbone / Harlan Collins / Joyce Everson
23. 7/24	Louise Lasser	The Preservation Hall Jazz Band
24. 7/31	Kris Kristofferson	Rita Coolidge
25. 9/18	Lily Tomlin	James Taylor
26. 9/25	Norman Lear	Boz Scaggs
27. 10/2	Eric Idle	Joe Cocker / Stuff
28. 10/16	Karen Black	John Prine
29. 10/23	Steve Martin	Kinky Friedman
30. 10/30	Buck Henry	The Band

The cast and guests say "Good night!" for another week. (Edie Baskin)

Show#, Date	*List of Hosts*	*Guest Artists*
31. 11/13	Dick Cavett	Ry Cooder
32. 11/20	Paul Simon	George Harrison
33. 11/27	Jodie Foster	Brian Wilson
34. 12/11	Candice Bergen	Frank Zappa
1977		
35. 1/15	Ralph Nader	George Benson / Andy Kaufman
36. 1/22	Ruth Gordon	Chuck Berry / Ricky Jay
37. 1/29	Fran Tarkenton	Leo Sayer / Donnie Harper & The Voices of Tomorrow
38. 2/26	Steve Martin	Lily Tomlin / The Kinks

Steve Martin has been a very popular host and works well with the rest of the cast. (Warner Bros. Records)

Show#, Date	List of Hosts	Guest Artists
39. 2/12	Sissy Spacek	Richard Baskin
40. 3/19	Broderick Crawford	The Meters / Dr. John / Levon Helm / Paul Butterfield
41. 3/26	Jack Burns	Santana
42. 4/9	Julian Bond	Tom Waits / Brick
43. 4/16	Elliot Gould	Roslyn Kind / McGarrigle Sisters
44. 4/23	Eric Idle	Alan Price / Neil Innes / Jeannette Charles
45. 5/14	Shelley Duvall	Joan Armatrading
46. 5/21	Buck Henry	Jennifer Warens / Kenny Vance
47. 9/24	Steve Martin	Jackson Browne
48. 10/8	Madeleine Kahn	Taj Mahal / Barry Humphries
49. 10/15	Hugh Hefner	Libby Titus / Andy Kaufman
50. 10/29	Charles Grodin	Paul Simon / The Persuasions
51. 11/12	Ray Charles	Franklyn Ajaye
52. 11/19	Buck Henry	Leon Redbone
53. 12/10	Mary Kay Place	Willie Nelson / Andy Kaufman
54. 12/17	Miskel Spillman	Elvis Costello
1978		
55. 1/21	Steve Martin	The Dirt Band / Randy Newman
56. 1/28	Robert Klein	Bonnie Raitt
57. 2/18	Chevy Chase	Billy Joel
58. 2/25	O.J. Simpson	Ashford & Simpson

Guest host O.J. Simpson gives some advice to Samurai Belushi. (Edie Baskin)

Show#, Date	*List of Hosts*	*Guest Artists*
59. 3/25	Art Garfunkel	Stephen Bishop / Andy Kaufman
60. 3/8	Jill Clayburgh	Eddie Money
61. 3/25	Christopher Lee	Meatloaf / Richard Belzer
62. 4/8	Michael Palin	Eugene Record
63. 4/15	Michael Sarrazin	Keith Jarrett / Gravity
64. 4/22	Steve Martin	The Blues Brothers
65. 5/13	Richard Dreyfuss	Jimmy Buffet / Gary Tigerman

Mick Jagger and the Rolling Stones appeared with New York City's Mayor, Ed Koch. (Edie Baskin)

Show #, Date	*List of Hosts*	*Guest Artists*
66. 5/20	Buck Henry	Sun Ra
67. 10/7	Mayor Ed Koch	The Rolling Stones
68. 10/14	Fred Willard	Devo
69. 10/21	Frank Zappa	—
70. 11/4	Steve Martin	Van Morrison
71. 11/11	Buck Henry	The Grateful Dead
72. 11/18	Carrie Fisher	The Blues Brothers
73. 12/2	Walter Matthau	Garrett Morris
74. 12/9	Eric Idle	Kate Bush
75. 12/16	Elliot Gould	Peter Tosh / Bob & Ray

DEVO is one of the newer bands to appear on SNL. (Warner Bros. Records)

SNL was one of the few television shows that David Byrne and the Talking Heads would appear on. (Michael McKenzie)

Show#, Date	List of Hosts	Guest Artists
1979		
76. 1/27	Michael Palin	The Doobie Brothers
77. 2/10	Cecily Tyson	The Talking Heads
78. 2/17	Rick Nelson	Judy Collins
79. 2/24	Kate Jackson	Andy Kaufman / Delbert McClinton
80. 3/10	Gary Busey	Eubie Blake / Gregory Hines
81. 3/17	Margot Kidder	The Chieftains
82. 4/7	Richard Benjamin	Rickie Lee Jones
83. 4/14	Milton Berle	Ornette Coleman
84. 5/12	Michael Palin	James Taylor
85. 5/19	Maureen Stapleton	Linda Ronstadt / Phoebe Snow
86. 5/26	Buck Henry	Bette Midler

GOOD NIGHT! SEE YOU NEXT WEEK! (Edie Baskin)